Critters of the Carolinas

Pocket Guide to Animals in Your State

ALEX TROUTMAN

produced in cooperation with

Wildlife Forever

About Wildlife Forever

Wildlife Forever works to conserve America's outdoor heritage through conservation education, preservation of habitat, and scientific management of fish and wildlife. Wildlife Forever is a 501c3 nonprofit organization dedicated to restoring habitat and teaching the next generation about conservation. Become a member and learn more about innovative programs like the Art of Conservation®, The Fish and Songbird Art Contests®, Clean Drain Dry Initiative™, and Prairie City USA®. For more information, visit wildlifeforever.org.

Thank you to Ann McCarthy, the original creator of the Critters series, for her dedication to wildlife conservation and to environmental education. Ann dedicates her work to her daughters, Megan and Katharine Anderson.

Front cover photos by **Karel Bock/shutterstock.com:** mink; **Ryan M. Bolton/shutterstock.com:** eastern hognose; **Harry Collins Photography/shutterstock.com:** belted kingfisher; Back cover photo by **Radiant Reptilia/shutterstock.com:** diamondback terrapin

Edited by Brett Ortler and Jenna Barron
Cover and book design by Jonathan Norberg
Proofreader: Emily Beaumont

10 9 8 7 6 5 4 3 2 1

Critters of the Carolinas

The first *Critters* books were produced by Wildlife Forever. AdventureKEEN is grateful for its continued partnership and advocacy on behalf of the natural world.

Published by Adventure Publications, an imprint of AdventureKEEN
310 Garfield Street South, Cambridge, Minnesota 55008
(800) 678-7006
www.adventurepublications.net

Printed in China
Cataloging-in-Publication data is available from the Library of Congress
ISBN 978-1-64755-554-2 (pbk.); 978-1-64755-555-9 (ebook)

Acknowledgments

I want to thank everyone who believed in and supported me over the years—a host of friends, family, and teachers. I want to especially thank my mom and my siblings Van, Bre, and TJ.

Dedication

I dedicate this book to my brother Van:
May you continue to enjoy the birds and wildlife in heaven.

This book is for all the kids who have a passion for nature and the outdoors, especially ones who identify as Black, Brown, Indigenous, and People of Color. May this be an encouragement to never give up. And if you have a dream and passion for something, pursue it relentlessly. I also hope to set an example that you can be successful as your full, authentic self!

Lastly, I dedicate this book to all those with ADHD and dyslexia, as well as all other members of the neurodivergent community. While our quirks make things more challenging, our goals are not impossible to reach; sometimes it takes a little more time and help, but we, too, can succeed!

Contents

Mammals

Birds

Reptiles and Amphibians

Introduction

My passion for nature started when I was young. I was always amazed by the sunlit fiery glow of the red-tailed hawks as they soared overhead when I went fishing with my family. The red-tailed hawk was my spark bird—the bird that captures your attention and gets you into birding. Through my many encounters with red-tailed hawks, and other species like garter snakes and coyotes, I found a passion for nature and the environment. Stumbling across conservationists like Steve Irwin, Jeff Corwin, and Jack Hanna introduced me to the field of Wildlife Biology as a career and gave birth to a dream that I was able to accomplish and live out: serving as a Fish and Wildlife Biologist for governmental agencies, as well as in the private sector.

My childhood dream was driven by a desire to learn more about the different types of ecosystems and the animals that call our wild places home. Books and field guides like this one whet my thirst for knowledge. Even before I could fully understand the words on the pages, I was drawn to books and flashcards that had animals on them. I could soon identify every animal I was shown and tell a fact about it. I hope that this edition of *Critters of the Carolinas* can be the fuel that sustains your passion for not only learning about wildlife, but also for caring for the environment and making sure that all are welcome in the outdoors. For others, may this book be the spark that ignites a flame for wildlife preservation and environmental stewardship. I hope that this book inspires children from lower socioeconomic and minority backgrounds to pursue their dreams to the fullest and be unapologetically themselves.

By profession, I'm a Fish and Wildlife Biologist, and I'm a nature enthusiast through and through. My love for nature includes making sure that everyone has an equal opportunity to enjoy the outdoors in their own way. So, as you use this book, I encourage you to be intentional in inviting others to appreciate nature with you. Enjoy your discoveries and stay curious!

–Alex Troutman

The Carolinas: The Tar Heel State and the Palmetto State

These two states share so much in common while still being completely different in so many ways. North Carolina is known for its industries and big cities, while South Carolina is more known for its cultural history and wonderfully wild coastlines. North Carolina was home to the first flight of Wilbur and Orville Wright, and South Carolina has an interesting naval history. However different, both Carolinas are made up of primarily forests, so they are very important for the lumber industry in the United States. They were first home to several Indigenous tribes including Cherokee and Creek. They were separated into North and South Carolina in 1710 when they were still British colonies.

While the states are different in many ways, they have very similar ecosystems filled with similar types of critters. The Appalachian Mountains span the western part of North Carolina, going down into the Blue Ridge Mountains in northwestern South Carolina. These mountain ranges are home to black bears, elk, and golden-winged warblers. The Piedmont is in both Carolinas (near the middle of North Carolina and two-thirds of South Carolina) and is made up of hills and plateaus. The Sand Hills are in the eastern part of South Carolina, and scientists believe that they were created by oceans back in ancient times. The Atlantic Coast to the east has sandy beaches and the Coastal Plains, where there are swamps and pine barrens teeming with many different animals, from alligators and snakes to beavers and black skimmers.

These environments are home to many animals, including dozens of mammal species in both states, more than 400 bird species on record in each, and more than 130 species of reptiles and amphibians each. And that's not to mention fish, countless insects and spiders, plants, and more. This is your guide to the animals, birds, reptiles, and amphibians that call the Carolinas home.

Some of North and South Carolina's most iconic plants, animals, and other natural resources are now officially recognized as state symbols. Get to know them below and see if you can spot them all! You'll probably encounter the state nicknames and mottos, so I've included them here too.

North Carolina

State Bird: northern cardinal

State Tree: pine

State Insect: honeybee

State Reptile: eastern box turtle

State Mammal: eastern gray squirrel

State Nickname: The Tar Heel State

State Motto: Esse quam videri *("To be, rather than to seem")*

South Carolina

State Bird: Carolina wren

State Tree: sabal palmetto

State Amphibian: spotted salamander

State Reptile: loggerhead sea turtle

State Animal: white-tailed deer

State Nickname: The Palmetto State

State Motto: Dum Spiro Sparo–Animis Opibusque Parati *("While I Breathe I Hope–Prepared in Mind and Resources")*

How to Use This Guide

This book is your introduction to some of the wonderful critters found in North and South Carolina; it includes 21 mammals, 27 birds, and 19 reptiles and amphibians. It includes some animals you probably already know, such as black bears and bald eagles, but others you may not know about, such as anhingas or green anoles. I've selected the species in this book because they are widespread (northern raccoon, page 36), abundant (white-tailed deer, page 50), or well-known but best observed from a safe distance (eastern copperhead, page 110).

The book is organized by types of animals: mammals, birds, and reptiles and amphibians. Within each section, the animals are in alphabetical order. If you'd like to look for a critter quickly, turn to the checklist (page 140), which you can also use to keep track of how many animals you've seen! For each species, you'll see a photo of the animal, along with neat facts and information on the animal's habitat, diet, its predators, how it raises its young, and more.

Safety Note

Nature can be unpredictable, so don't go outdoors alone, and always tell an adult when you're going outside. All wild animals should be treated with respect. If you see one—big or small—don't get close to it or attempt to touch or feed it. Instead, keep your distance and enjoy spotting it. If you can, snap some pictures with a camera or make a quick drawing using a sketchbook. If the animal is getting too close, is acting strangely, or seems sick or injured, tell an adult right away, as it might have rabies, a disease that can affect mammals. The good news is there's a rabies vaccine, so it's important to visit a doctor right away if you get bit or scratched by a wild animal.

Notes About Icons

Each species page includes basic information about an animal, from what it eats to how it survives the winter. The book also includes information that's neat to know; in the mammals section, each page includes a simple track illustration of the animal, with approximate track size included. And along the bottom, there is an example track pattern for the mammal, with the exception for those that primarily glide or fly (flying squirrels and bats).

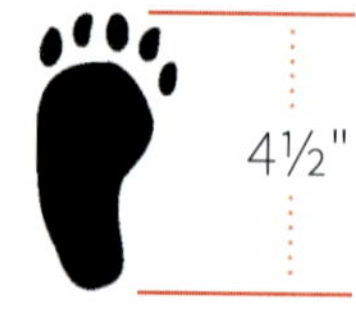

On the left-hand page for each mammal, a rough-size illustration is included that shows how big the animal is when compared to a basketball.

Also on the left-hand page, there are icons that tell you when each animal is most active: nocturnal (at night), diurnal (during the day), or crepuscular (at dawn/dusk), so you know when to look. If an animal has a "zzz" icon, it hibernates during the winter. Some animals hibernate every winter, and their internal processes (breathing and heartbeat) slow down almost entirely. Other animals only partially hibernate, but this still helps them save energy and survive through the coldest part of the year.

nocturnal
(active at night)

diurnal
(active during day)

crepuscular
(most active at dawn and dusk)

hibernates/deep sleeper
(dormant during winter)

ground nest

cup nest

platform nest

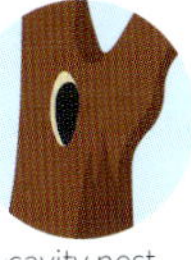
cavity nest

migrates

On the left-hand side of each bird page, the nest for the species is shown, along with information on whether or not the bird migrates; on the right-hand side, there's information on where it goes.

Did you know?

Beavers are rodents! Yes, these flat-tailed mammals are rodents, like rats and squirrels. In fact, they are the largest native rodents in North America. Just like other rodents, beavers have large incisors, which they use to chew through trees to build dams and dens. Beavers are the original wetland engineers. By damming rivers and streams, beavers create ponds and wetlands.

Size Comparison

Most Active

Track Size

American Beaver

Castor canadensis

Size: Body is 25–30 inches long; tail is 9–13 inches long; weighs 30–70 pounds

Habitat: Wooded wetland areas near ponds, streams, and lakes

Range: Beavers can be found throughout North and South Carolina and the majority of the US.

Food: Leaves, twigs, and stems; they also feed on fruits and aquatic plant roots. Throughout the year they gather and store tree cuttings, which they eat in winter.

Den: A beaver's home is called a lodge. It consists of a pile of branches that is splattered with mud and vegetation. Lodges are constructed on the banks of lakes and streams and have exits and entrances that are underwater.

Young: Young beavers (kits) are born in late April through May and June in litters of 3–4. After two years they are considered mature and will be forced out of the den.

Predators: Bobcats, cougars, bears, wolves, and coyotes. Human trappers are major predators too.

Tracks: A beaver's front foot looks a lot like your hand; it has five fingers. The hind (back) foot is long, with five separate toes that have webbing or extra skin between them.

Beavers range from dark brown to reddish brown. They have a stocky body with hind legs that are longer than the front legs. The beaver's body is covered in dense fur, but its tail is naked and has special blood vessels that help it cool or warm its body.

Did you know?

It's a common misconception that bats are blind, but, in fact, they can see. However, they still rely on a special technique called echolocation to find food and to travel throughout the night sky. A female bat of reproductive age can eat her own body weight in insects in a single night. She does so while eating on the wing, meaning eating while in flight.

Size Comparison

Most Active

Hibernates

Big Brown Bat

Eptesicus fuscus

Size: 4–5 inches long; wingspan is 12–16 inches; weighs ½–1 ounce

Habitat: Cities, forests, deserts, mountains, and meadows

Range: Big brown bats are found statewide in South Carolina. They can also be found in north-central areas of Canada, throughout the US into Mexico, Central America, and northern areas of South America.

Food: Insectivorous (insect eater); beetles make up most of their diet. They also feed on flies, wasps, and moths.

Den: Roosts in a nursing colony that may contain 40–100 or more pregnant females. Reproductive males, or bachelors, usually roost alone or in small groups. Bats roost in mines, tree cavities, under bridges and other human-made structures, and in rock crevices.

Young: Young bats (pups) are born blind, without fur, between May and June. Pups will feed on milk for approximately 4–5 weeks. They will start the process of learning to fly at around 3–5 weeks and become independent a couple of weeks later.

Predators: Snakes, owls, raccoons, feral cats, and humans

Tracks: Though they are rarely on the ground to leave a track, it would show as one thumbprint from the forearm and a hind footprint.

Big brown bats are large and have a furry back that's glossy brown to earthy red. They have a light-brown belly, hairless black wings, and rounded ears. In winter, they hibernate in tree cavities, human-made structures, and rock crevices. They maintain temperatures above 31 degrees and up to 42 degrees.

The big brown bat does not often leave tracks.

Did you know?

Female bears weigh between 90 and 300 pounds and are smaller than the average adult human male in the US. But don't let their small size fool you; with a bite force around 800 pounds per square inch (PSI) and a swiping force of over 400 pounds, these bears are not to be taken lightly.

Size Comparison

Most Active

Track Size

Hibernates

Black Bear

Ursus americanus

Size: 5–6 feet long (nose to tail); weighs 90–600 pounds

Habitat: Forests, mountains, lowland areas, and swamps

Range: They are found in much of North America, from northern Canada down into Mexico. They can be found in both North and South Carolina in the eastern coastal counties near swamplands and in more mountainous areas in the western part of the states. In the middle of South Carolina, the population is transient (or just passing through the state).

Food: Berries, fish, crops, small mammals, wild grapes, tree shoots, ants, bees, and even deer fawns

Den: Denning usually starts in December, with bears emerging in late March or April. Dens can be either dug (out of a hillside, for example) or constructed with materials such as leaves, grass, and moss.

Young: Two cubs are usually born at one time (a litter), often in January. Cubs are born blind and without fur, with pink skin. They weigh 8–16 ounces.

Predators: Humans and other bears. Sometimes, other carnivores, such as mountain lions, wolves, coyotes, or even bobcats, will prey on black bears. Cubs are especially vulnerable.

Tracks: Front print is usually 4–6 inches long and 3½–5 inches wide, with the hind foot being 6–7 inches long and 3½–5 inches wide. The feet have five toes.

Black bears are usually black in color, but they can be many different variations of black and brown. Some even have grayish, reddish, or blond fur.

Did you know?

Coyotes are the biggest group of large predators in North and South Carolina. At one time, coyotes were only found in the central and western parts of the US, but now, with the help of humans (eliminating predators and clearing forests), they can be found throughout most of the country.

Size Comparison Most Active Track Size

Coyote

Canis latrans

Size: 3–4 feet long; weighs 21–50 pounds

Habitat: Urban and suburban areas, woodlands, grasslands, and farm fields

Range: They are found throughout the US and Mexico, the northern parts of Central America, and southern Canada. They can be found statewide in both North and South Carolina.

Food: A variety of prey, including rodents, birds, deer, and sometimes livestock

Den: Coyotes will dig their own dens but will often use old fox or badger dens or hollow logs.

Young: 5–7 pups, independent around 8–10 months

Predators: Bears and wolves; humans trap and kill for pelts and to "protect" livestock.

Tracks: Four toes and a carpal pad (the single pad below the toe pads) can be seen on all four feet.

Coyotes have brown, reddish-brown, or gray back fur with a lighter gray-to-white belly. They have a longer muzzle than other wild canines. They are active mostly during the night (nocturnal) but also during the twilight and dawn hours (crepuscular).

Did you know?

Chipmunks get their English name from the "chip" or alert calls they use when they sense a threat. Eastern chipmunks are not fully herbivores (plant eaters); in fact, they eat a variety of things, including other mammals and amphibians, like frogs.

Size Comparison

Most Active

Track Size

Hibernates

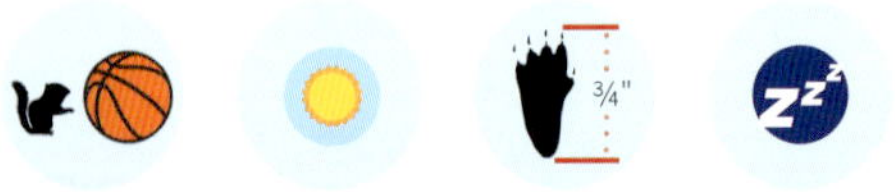

Eastern Chipmunk

Tamias striatus

Size: Body is 3–6 inches long; tail is 3–4 inches long; weighs 2½–5½ ounces

Habitat: Suburban areas, woodlands, and dense scrub areas

Range: In North Carolina, they can be found in the majority of the state, from western to central areas, in the mountains, Piedmont, and Coastal Plain. In South Carolina, they are found in the westernmost counties of the state. They're found throughout the eastern US, and in southern Canada.

Food: Berries, nuts, seeds, frogs, insects

Den: Has multiple chambers (or rooms); the entrance is usually hidden under brush, fallen trees, rock piles, and human-made landscaping items.

Young: 2–8 young (kits) per litter, 2 litters per year. Born blind and without fur. Weigh under an ounce at birth. Eyes open at 4 weeks, becomes independent at 8 weeks

Predators: Coyotes, feral and outdoor house cats, snakes, weasels, bobcats, hawks, and owls

Tracks: The front foot has four digit (toe) pads and is ½ inch long; the hind foot has five digit pads and is just under ¾ inch.

Chipmunks are small rodents with brown base colors, seven alternating stripes, and white bellies. During winter, they will stay underground. They hide food in underground caches that they will feed on through the winter.

Did you know?

The eastern cottontail gets its name from its short, puffy tail that looks like a cotton ball. A cottontail can travel up to 18 miles per hour! Rabbits have great hearing and eyesight. They can almost see all the way around them (360 degrees). On days with high wind, they will bed down in a burrow because the wind interferes with their ability to hear and detect predators.

Size Comparison

Most Active

Track Size

Eastern Cottontail

Sylvilagus floridanus

Size: 16–19 inches long; weighs 1½–4 pounds

Habitat: Forests, swamps, orchards, deserts, and farm areas

Range: Found throughout the eastern US to Arizona and New Mexico. They are found throughout the states of North and South Carolina.

Food: Clovers; grasses; wild strawberries; garden plants; and twigs of a variety of trees, including maple, oak, and sumac

Den: Rabbits don't dig dens; they bed in shallow, grassy, saucer-shaped depressions (holes) or under shrubs. They will sometimes use woodchuck dens in the winter.

Young: They usually have 2–4 kits at one time, but it's not uncommon to have 7 or more. Born naked and blind, they weigh about an ounce (about the same weight as a slice of bread) and gain weight very quickly.

Predators: Owls, coyotes, eagles, weasels, humans, and foxes

Tracks: The front foot is an inch long with four toe pads; the hind foot is 3½ inches long.

An eastern cottontail sports thick brown fur with a white belly, a gray rump, and a white "cotton" tail. During the winter, it survives by eating bark off of fruit trees and shrubs.

Did you know?

The eastern fox squirrel's bones appear pink under ultraviolet (UV) light, a type of light human eyes can't see. Squirrels accidentally help plant trees by forgetting where they have previously buried nuts. Sometimes, they seem to pretend to bury nuts to throw off would-be nut thieves.

Size Comparison

Most Active

Track Size

Eastern Fox Squirrel

Sciurus niger

Size: 19–28 inches long; weighs 1–3 pounds

Habitat: Open woodlands, suburban areas, and dense forests

Range: They are found throughout the eastern US to Texas and as far north as the Dakotas. In North Carolina, they can be found throughout most of the state, especially in the central and eastern areas in the mountains, Sand Hills, Coastal Plain, and the Piedmont. In South Carolina, their population is spotted throughout the state in the coastal region, with some populations being observed in the Piedmont area.

Food: Acorns, seeds, nuts, insects such as moths and beetles, birds, eggs, and dead fish

Den: Ball-shaped dreys, or nests, are made of vegetation like leaves, sometimes in tree cavities.

Young: 2–3 kits are born between December and February and May and June. Kittens are born naked and weigh half an ounce; they are cared for by their parents for the first 7–8 weeks. They can reproduce by around 10–11 months for males and 8 months for females.

Predators: Humans, hawks, cats, coyotes, bobcats, and weasels

Tracks: The front tracks have four digits (toes), and the hind feet have five digits.

The eastern fox squirrel is the largest tree squirrel in Alabama. It is gray or reddish brown with a yellowish or light-brown underside. There are also rare black and smoky-gray phases. Both the male and female look the same.

Did you know?

Eastern gray squirrels are the most common species in the Carolinas and are the most abundant squirrel species in the eastern US; in fact, there may be as many as 20 squirrels living in just 1 acre of forest. They use both their sense of smell and memory to find their buried caches or storage of food.

Size Comparison

Most Active

Track Size

Eastern Gray Squirrel

Sciurus carolinensis

Size: 5–7 inches long (15–20 inches with tail); weighs ¾–1½ pounds

Habitat: Hardwood forests, residential areas, city parks, suburban and urban woodlands

Range: They can be found from eastern Canada to as far south as Florida and as far west as North Dakota. They are found statewide in North and South Carolina.

Food: They are omnivores that eat a variety of foods, including nuts, acorns, seeds, fruit, tree buds, insects, and sometimes even bird eggs and young birds.

Den: They nest in the cavity of trees or build nests called dreys out of leaves and place them in the forks of limbs or human-made structures.

Young: 2–4 kits are born after around 45 days; the first litter is born between February and March and a second litter between June and August.

Predators: Snakes, pet cats and dogs, bobcats, red foxes, weasels, minks, and humans who hunt them for meat

Tracks: Both feet have five toes and a carpal pad. The front foot is 1¼–1⅞ inches long by ¾–1¾ inches wide, and the hind foot is 1¼–2 inches long by 1–1¾ inches wide.

Gray squirrels are rodents, like rats and mice. They have a bushy tail that is pale gray to silver. They have a gray back, though it can vary in color from reddish brown to black or white. They have a white underside or belly area.

Did you know?

Elk are known to be the loudest of all cervids (Deer family). Males produce a low-pitched bellow or roar, called a bugle. Bugling is a technique that involves both roaring and whistling at the same time. Elk use their bugle or bugling to attract mates or announce territories during the fall mating season. Their bugles can be heard over long distances.

Size Comparison

Most Active

Track Size

Elk

Cervus elaphus canadensis

Size: 5–8 feet tall; weighs 377–1,095 pounds

Habitat: Open woodlands, mountain areas, shrublands, coniferous swamps, and hardwood forests

Range: Found throughout the western US, portions of the Southeast, and in Canada. They were once native to both Carolinas, but today, they are only found in North Carolina in the southern Appalachian Mountains.

Food: Elk are herbivores that eat grasses; flowers; and leaves from trees like cedar, red maple, and basswood.

Den: No den; mother elk will hide young calves in tall grasses.

Young: Calves are born after 240–265 days. At birth, calves weigh around 30 pounds and have spots through the first summer. Separation from mother's milk happens around the 60-day mark, but calves will continue to get care and protection from mom for around a year. They reach full maturity around 16 months.

Predators: Mountain lions, Mexican gray wolves, and bears. Calves may fall victim to bobcats and coyotes.

Tracks: Front tracks of an adult are about 4¾ inches long and wide. Hind foot tracks are 4½ inches long and 3½ inches wide. Two toes are on each foot.

Elk come in different shades of browns and tans. In the summer and spring, they are lighter brown to tan; in the winter they are a deep dark brown. During both seasons, they have a cream or off-white rump. They sport a darker tone on the head, neck, belly, and legs.

Did you know?

Gray foxes are the only members of the Dog family in the US that can climb trees well. They have semi-retractable claws, almost like cats, enabling them to hang onto trees.

Size Comparison

Most Active

Track Size

Gray Fox

Urocyon cinereoargenteus

Size: 2½–3½ feet long; weighs 6–10 pounds

Habitat: Forests, grasslands, urban (city) areas, and brushy and scrub-heavy areas near water sources

Range: They are found in much of the continental US. They can be found throughout North and South Carolina.

Food: Omnivorous (eating both plants and animals, including birds, insects, mice, and rabbits). Also eats apples, nuts, grasses, various berries, and corn

Den: Usually only dens during mating season. Sometimes they use abandoned dens of other animals that they will widen or extend; also use hollowed-out trees and cavities, caves, and crevices in rocky areas.

Young: Kits or pups, sometimes called cubs, are born in April or May; litters of 4–5 young are born at one time; young feed on milk for approximately 3 weeks and are then fed solids. At around 4 months they learn to hunt, and they eventually leave the family around the 10-month mark.

Predators: Bobcats, great horned owls, coyotes, and humans

Tracks: Front paw is 1¾–2 inches long and 1¾ inches wide. Hind foot is 1½ inches long and 1¼–1¾ inches wide.

Males are a bit larger than females. Fur comes in various mixtures of reds, grays, white, and black. The breast, belly, and side areas are a brownish red. The head is salt-and-pepper (mixture of gray, white, and black) with a white muzzle or nose area, cheeks, and throat. The tail has a distinctive black stripe that runs to the tip and bushes out.

Did you know?

Weasels are small but tough! They will attack prey over three times their own size, and they help control rodent and pest species by eating mice, voles, and other small mammals.

Size Comparison

Most Active

Track Size

Long-tailed Weasel

Mustela frenata

Size: 14–18 inches long; weighs 5 ounces to 1 pound

Habitat: Forests, farms, and rocky areas

Range: Weasels can be found throughout the United States, except for a small pocket in southern California, Nevada, and Arizona. They are found throughout North Carolina, but due to their secretive lifestyle, they are not frequently seen. In South Carolina, they have a scattered range with most being observed in the Piedmont region.

Food: Ducks and other birds, frogs, rodents, rabbits, and sometimes domesticated chickens and eggs; they will hide extra food to eat later.

Den: Weasels will dig dens but will also use rock piles, abandoned burrows of other animals, or hollow logs. Dens are covered with fur and grass.

Young: 4–8 kits are born in April; they reach adult weight within 4 months.

Predators: Hawks, owls, coyotes, foxes, humans, and cats

Tracks: The front foot is wider than the hind foot. Each foot has five toe pads with four claws extending from them.

Long-tailed weasels have several color phases, including alternating from brown to white as the seasons change from summer to winter.

Did you know?

Mink have webbed feet, like otters. Although they usually dive and swim short distances, mink can dive over 13 feet deep and swim for over 95 feet underwater, if necessary!

Size Comparison

Most Active

Track Size

Mink

Mustela vison

Size: 16–27 inches long; weighs 1½–3½ pounds

Habitat: Wetland areas with dense vegetation near streams, lakes, and swamps

Range: They are found throughout most of the US and Canada. They are found statewide in both Carolinas, though they are rarely seen in South Carolina; they are found more in the upper Piedmont regions and the southern marshes of the coastal region.

Food: Fish, eggs, snakes, muskrats, farm animals, small mammals, and aquatic animals such as crawfish

Den: Their dens are near water, in holes in the ground, hollow logs, and old muskrat and beaver lodges; they will use grass or fur from prey as bedding.

Young: At birth, they weigh less than an ounce; mothers give birth to 3–6 young, called kits. They are mature at 1 year old.

Predators: Otters, birds of prey, wolves, coyotes, bobcats, internal parasites, and humans (who trap them for fur)

Tracks: Both the front and hind tracks resemble a gloved hand. Both the left and right tracks are seen parallel to each other because the mink often bound (leap) when moving. Tracks are usually seen near water.

A mostly nocturnal (active at night) animal, it has a shiny or glossy dark-brown coat that it keeps all year long. Mink usually have a white or pale-yellow chest patch or bib on the throat that sometimes extends to the belly.

Did you know?

The raccoon is great at catching fish and other aquatic animals, such as mussels and crawfish. They are also excellent swimmers, but they apparently avoid swimming because the water makes their fur heavy. Raccoons can turn their feet 180 degrees; this helps them when climbing, especially when going headfirst down trees.

Size Comparison

Most Active

Track Size

Hibernates

Northern Raccoon

Procyon lotor

Size: 24–40 inches long; weighs 15–28 pounds

Habitat: Woody areas, grasslands, suburban and urban areas, wetlands, and marshes

Range: They are found throughout the US; they are also found in Mexico and southern Canada. They are found throughout North and South Carolina, mostly near the coast.

Food: Eggs, insects, garbage, garden plants, berries, nuts, fish, carrion, small mammals, and aquatic invertebrates like crawfish and mussels

Den: Raccoon dens are built in hollow trees, abandoned burrows, caves, and human-made structures.

Young: 2–6 young (kits) are born around March through July. They are born weighing 2 ounces, are around 4 inches long, and are blind with lightly colored fur.

Predators: Coyotes, foxes, bobcats, humans, and even large birds of prey

Tracks: Their front tracks resemble human handprints. The back tracks sort of look like human footprints.

The northern raccoon has dense fur with variations of brown, black, and white streaks. It has black, mask-like markings on its face and a black-and-gray/brownish ringed tail. During the fall, it will grow a thick layer of fat to stay warm in the winter.

Did you know?

Otters are good swimmers and can close their nostrils while diving. This allows them to dive for as long as 8 minutes and to depths of over 50 feet. Otter fur is the thickest of all mammal fur. River otters have an incredible 67,000 hairs for every square centimeter!

Size Comparison

Most Active

Track Size

Northern River Otter

Lontra canadensis

Size: 29–48 inches long; weighs 10–33 pounds

Habitat: Lakes, marshes, rivers, and large streams; suburban areas

Range: Otters can be found statewide in the Carolinas. They are found across much of the US, except parts of the Southwest and portions of the central US.

Food: Fish, frogs, snakes, crabs, crawfish, mussels, birds, eggs, turtles, and small mammals. They sometimes eat aquatic vegetation too.

Den: They den in burrows along the river, usually under rocks, riverbanks, hollow trees, and vegetation.

Young: 2–4 young (pups) are born between November and May. Pups are born with their eyes closed. They will leave the area at around 6 months old and reach full maturity at around 2 or 3 years.

Predators: Alligators, coyotes, bobcats, bears, and dogs

Tracks: Their feet have nonretractable claws and are webbed.

Northern river otters have thick, dark-brown fur and a long, slender body. Their fur is made up of two types: a short undercoat and a coarse top coat that repels water. They have webbed feet and a layer of fat that helps keep them warm in cold water.

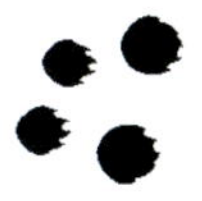

Did you know?

Flying squirrels don't actually fly! Instead, they use special folds of skin to glide through the air. They can glide over 100 feet at a time. They have thick paws that aid them in landing. Because they move from tree to tree, they help to spread seeds and fungi. The northern flying squirrel in North Carolina is a super-rare subspecies.

Size Comparison

Most Active

Track Size

Northern/Southern Flying Squirrel

Glaucomys sabrinus/Glaucomys volans

Size: 9 inches long; weighs 2–3 ounces

Habitat: Forests with older trees, northern flying squirrels are found more in forested mountains.

Range: Northern: found from Alaska to the northeastern coast and a few Appalachian states; only in western NC. Southern: found throughout the eastern US and parts of Mexico; statewide in SC.

Food: Nuts, berries, acorns, small birds, mice, insects, and mushrooms

Den: They make nests in tree hollows. They will also use abandoned woodpecker holes and human-made nest boxes or birdhouses. They line the nest with chewed bark, grasses, moss, and feathers.

Young: 2–5 young (kits) are born per litter; they drink milk from the mother for around 70 days and will be fully independent at around 4 months and mature at around a year old.

Predators: Small hawks, foxes, owls, martens, and weasels

Tracks: Tracks are rare because they spend most of their time in trees.

The flying squirrel is a grayish brown nocturnal (active at night) animal that glides through the air from tree to tree. The patagium, or skin fold, stretches from their ankles to their wrist, allowing them to "fly." (People have even built similar "squirrel suits" to glide with, and they've worked!) During winter months, flying squirrels share cavities with others.

Did you know?

The red fox is a great jumper and can leap over 13 feet in one bound. Red foxes are also fast, as they can run up to 30 miles per hour. Red foxes, like wild cats, will hide their food to eat later, often under leaf litter or in holes.

Size Comparison

Most Active

Track Size

Red Fox

Vulpes vulpes

Size: 37–42 inches long; weighs 8–15 pounds

Habitat: Grasslands, forest edges, farm fields, and suburban areas

Range: Red foxes can be found in nearly all of the US, except for the Southwest. They can be found statewide in both North and South Carolina.

Food: Omnivores (they eat both meat and plants); they eat frogs, birds, snakes, small mammals, insects, seeds, nuts, and fruit.

Den: They dig underground dens, sometimes several at once, splitting a litter (babies) between the two. They also use old badger or groundhog holes or tree roots for den sites.

Young: 3–7 young (kits) are born; pups will nurse (drink milk from the mother) for around 10 weeks and will become independent at around 7 months.

Predators: Coyotes, lynx, cougars, and other species of carnivores. Humans trap and hunt foxes for fur.

Tracks: Their footprints resemble dog tracks and have four toe pads; they walk in a line with the hind foot behind the front.

The red fox is a medium-size predator with a burnt orange or rust-like red coat with a bushy, white-tipped tail. The legs are usually black or grayish. The red fox's tail is about one third of its body length.

Did you know?

One of the most endangered species of wolf in the world and one of the rarest mammals, there are fewer than 20 individual red wolves in the wild. They can eat 2–5 pounds of food daily and can run over 45 miles per hour.

Size Comparison

Most Active

Track Size

Red Wolf

Canis lupus rufus

Size: 4–5 feet long; 2 feet tall at the shoulder; weighs 45–85 pounds

Habitat: Coastal areas, forest swamps, and farmlands

Range: At one time, the range extended from Pennsylvania down to Florida and as far west as Texas. Today, they are only found on the Albemarle-Pamlico Peninsula in North Carolina.

Food: Deer, rabbits, rodents, raccoons, and the non-native nutria

Den: Dens are made in hollow tree trunks, abandoned dens from other animals, and along stream banks.

Young: Pups are born in late spring with eyes closed. Pups start to venture away from den at around 6 weeks and will be adult sized at around 1 year. They reach reproductive maturity at around 3 years.

Predators: They are apex predators (meaning the top of the food chain). Humans and other wild dog species like coyotes will kill them to defend their territory.

Tracks: Front paws are 3–4¼ inches long by 2⅛–3 inches wide; hind prints are slightly smaller than the front.

Slender members of the Canine family, red wolves have brown or buffy-colored fur with black striping down their back. Their bushy tails have a black tip. Their muzzle or nose, area behind their ears, and back of their legs are red. They have a shorter, stouter mouth compared to coyotes, and their ears are larger than both gray wolves and coyotes.

Did you know?

Tricolored bats got their name because of the three different colors of fur on their back: dark gray on the bottom, golden-brown in the middle, and brown or earth-tone red on the top.

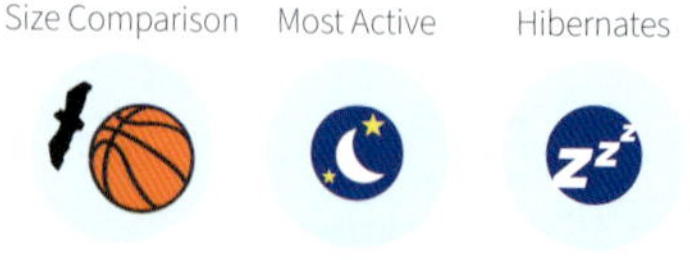

Size Comparison

Most Active

Hibernates

Tricolored Bat

Perimyotis subflavus

Size: 3–3½ inches long; wingspan is 8⅓–10⅓ inches; weighs 1⁄10–¾ ounce or about as much as a quarter

Habitat: Forests, caves, urban (city) areas, grasslands, and orchards

Range: Widespread across the eastern and central US as far west as Texas. They are found statewide in both North and South Carolina.

Food: Mosquitoes, beetles, ants, moths, and cicadas

Den: Roost in trees, buildings, culverts (sewage drains), caves, and in Spanish moss. Females will roost in colonies of 25 or more individuals. Males are solitary and do not have bachelor colonies like other bat species. Bats mate in the fall and give birth in the spring.

Young: Pups are born blind and furless in June and July. Pups learn to fly 3 weeks after birth, and within a month they are able to hunt for themselves. They are mature by their first fall but will not usually mate until their second fall.

Predators: Owls, raccoons, snakes, and hawks

Tracks: Though they are rarely on the ground to leave a track, it would show as one thumbprint from the forearm and a hind footprint.

Tricolored bats are a golden hue of yellowish and brown fur. Single hairs are darkly shaded at the bottom, yellow hued in the midsection, and brown at the tip. This is the reason for the name "tricolored." During the winter they hibernate in caves, mines, and rock crevices. In areas with a lack of caves or mines, they hibernate in roadside culverts.

The tricolored bat does not often leave tracks.

Did you know?

The opossum is the only marsupial native to the US. Marsupials are a special group of animals that are most well-known for their pouches, which they use to carry their young. When frightened, young opossums will play dead (called playing possum) and adults will show their teeth and hiss or run away.

Size Comparison

Most Active

Track Size

Virginia Opossum

Didelphis virginiana

Size: 22–45 inches long; weighs 4–8 pounds

Habitat: Forests, woodlands, meadows, and suburban areas

Range: They are found throughout the eastern US, Canada, and also in Mexico and Costa Rica. They can be found statewide in both North and South Carolina.

Food: Eggs, small mammals, garbage, insects, worms, birds, fruit, and occasionally small reptiles and amphibians

Den: They den in hollow trees, abandoned animal burrows, and buildings.

Young: A litter of 6–20 young (joeys) are born blind and without fur; their limbs are not fully formed. Young will climb from the birthing area into the mother's pouch and stay until 8 weeks old; they then alternate between the mother's pouch and her back for 4 weeks. At 12 weeks they are independent.

Predators: Hawks, owls, pet cats and dogs, coyotes, and bobcats

Tracks: The front feet are 2 inches long and around 1½ inches wide and resemble a child's hands; the hind feet are 2½ inches long and around 2¼ inches wide; they have fingers in front with a fifth finger that acts as a thumb.

The Virginia opossum has long gray-and-black fur; the face is white, and the tail is pink to gray and furless. Opossums have long claws.

Did you know?

When they first emerge, a deer's antlers are covered in a special skin called velvet. Deer can run up to 40 miles per hour and can jump over 8 feet vertically (high) and over 15 feet horizontally (across).

Size Comparison

Most Active

Track Size

White-tailed Deer

Odocoileus virginianus

Size: 4–6 feet long; 3–4 feet tall at front shoulder; weighs 114–308 pounds

Habitat: Forest edges, brushy fields, woody farmlands, prairies, and swamps

Range: They are found throughout the US, except for much of the Southwest; they are also found in southern Canada and into South America. They are found throughout North and South Carolina.

Food: Fruits, grasses, tree shrubs, nuts, and bark

Den: Deer do not den but will bed down in tall grasses and shrubby areas.

Young: Deer usually give birth to twins (fawns) that are 3–6 pounds in late May to June. The fawns are born with spots; this coloration helps them hide in vegetation. Young become independent at 1–2 years.

Predators: Wolves, coyotes, bears, bobcats, and humans

Tracks: Both front and hind feet have two teardrop- or comma-shaped toes.

Crepuscular (active at dawn and dusk), white-tailed deer have big brown eyes with eye rings and a long snout with a black, glossy nose. The males have antlers, which fall off each year. All deer have a white tail that they flash upward when alarmed. Deer molt or change fur color twice a year. They sport rusty-brown fur in the summer; in early fall, they transition to winter coats that are grayish brown in color.

Did you know?

Anhingas often soar high up in the sky in groups called "kettles," often with raptors. The anhinga is less buoyant (floats less easily) than other birds, so its body sits lower in the water with its head and neck sticking out, making it easy to mistake for a snake. This is why it is sometimes called the snake bird.

Nest Type

Most Active

Migrates

Anhinga

Anhinga anhinga

Size: 28½–37½ inches long; wingspan of 43 inches; weighs 45–48 ounces

Habitat: Shallow areas of freshwater marshes, swamps, mangroves, lagoons, and rivers

Range: Can be found year-round in the eastern coastal areas of the US. In North and South Carolina, they are breeding residents.

Food: Mostly fish, but they also feed on aquatic (water-living) insects, crawfish, and shrimp. Sometimes they will take on snakes, alligator hatchlings, and baby turtles.

Nesting: Nesting takes place in colonies, or rookeries, of other water-loving birds. Parents share care duties.

Nest: Platform nests are constructed mostly by the female with the male supplying sticks and twigs; the inside is usually lined with grasses and leaves.

Eggs: 2–5 palish-white-to-blue eggs about 2–2½ inches long and 1½ inches wide

Young: Eggs hatch 25–30 days after laying. Chicks are born with eyes open and featherless. Young will leap out of the nest in the presence of danger.

Predators: Snakes, squirrels, owls, common ravens, blue jays, red-bellied woodpeckers, and a variety of hawks

Migration: They migrate to the Carolinas from areas in Florida, Georgia, the Caribbean, and South America during the spring and leave during the fall.

Males are black with whitish to silver streaking on the back and wings. Juveniles and females have a light-brown-to-tan head and body. Both sexes have orange-yellow feet, legs, and bill.

Did you know?

The bald eagle is an endangered species success story! The bald eagle was once endangered due to a pesticide called DDT that weakened eggshells and caused them to crack early. Through the banning of DDT and other conservation efforts, the bald eagle population recovered, and it was removed from the Endangered Species List in July of 2007.

Nest Type

Most Active

Bald Eagle

Haliaeetus leucocephalus

Size: 3½ feet long; wingspan of 6½–8 feet; weighs 8–14 pounds

Habitat: Forests and tree stands (small forests) near river edges, lakes, seashores, and wetlands

Range: They are found throughout much of the US.

Food: Fish, waterfowl (ducks), rabbits, squirrels, muskrats, and deer carcasses; will steal food from other eagles or ospreys

Nesting: Eagles have lifelong partners that begin nesting in fall, laying eggs November–February.

Nest: They build a large nest out of sticks, high up in trees; the nest can be over 5 feet wide and over 6 feet tall, often shaped like an upside-down cone.

Eggs: 1–3 white eggs

Young: Young (chicks) will hatch at around 35 days; young will leave the nest at around 12 weeks. It takes up to 5 years for eagles to get that iconic look!

Predators: Few; collisions with cars sometimes occur.

Migration: In the Carolinas, many eagles do not migrate at all.

Adult bald eagles have a dark-brown body, a white head and tail, and a golden-yellow beak. Juvenile eagles are mostly brown at first, but their color pattern changes over their first few years. A bald eagle can use its wings as oars to propel itself across bodies of water.

Did you know?

The barred owl has dark-brown eyes; many other owls have yellow eyes. Barred owls, like other owls, have special structures on their primary feathers that allow them to fly silently through the air.

Nest Type

Most Active

Barred Owl

Strix varia

Size: 17–20 inches long; wingspan of 3½ feet; weighs 2 pounds

Habitat: Forested areas, near floodplains of lakes and rivers

Range: They can be found throughout the eastern US and southern Canada, with scattered populations throughout the Pacific Northwest. They are found throughout the states of North and South Carolina.

Food: Squirrels, rabbits, and mice; will also prey on birds and aquatic animals like frogs, fish, and crawfish

Nesting: Courtship starts in late fall; nesting starts in winter.

Nest: They use hollow trees; they will also use abandoned nests of other animals and human-made nest structures.

Eggs: 2–4 white eggs with a rough shell

Young: Young (chicks) hatch between 27 and 33 days; they have white down feathers and leave the nest around 5 weeks after hatching. They are fully independent at around 6 months and fully mature at around 2 years.

Predators: Great horned owls, raccoons, weasels, and sometimes northern goshawks feed on eggs and young in the nest.

Migration: Barred owls do not migrate.

The barred owl is a medium-size bird with dark rings highlighting the face. Their feathers are brown and grayish, often with streaking or a bar-like pattern. They have no ear tufts and have a rounded head with a yellow beak and brown eyes. They can easily be identified by their call: "Who cooks for you, who cooks for you all?"

Did you know?

Kingfishers inspired human technology! Bullet trains around the world are designed after the kingfisher's beak, which allows it to dive into water without a splash. This design was used in bullet trains to allow them to enter into tunnels without making a large booming sound. This process of modeling human technology after animal features is called biomimicry.

Most Active

Belted Kingfisher

Megaceryle alcyon

Size: 11–13¾ inches long; wingspan is 19–24 inches; weighs 5–6 ounces

Habitat: Forests and grassland areas near rivers, ponds, lakes

Range: Year-round residents that can be found throughout most of the US and Canada

Food: Carnivores, they eat mostly fish and other aquatic animals, such as crawfish and frogs, and occasionally other birds, mammals, and berries.

Nesting: Nests are in the form of upward-sloped burrows that are dug in soft banks on or near water. (The upward slopes prevent flooding.)

Nest: Females and males select the nest site together; males do most of the digging.

Eggs: 5–8 white, smooth, glossy eggs are laid per clutch (group of eggs).

Young: Chicks are born featherless with pink skin, closed eyes, and a dark bill. They receive care from both parents. Chicks leave the nest after about 28 days.

Predators: Snakes, hawks, and mammals

Migration: They do not migrate.

The belted kingfisher is bluish gray on top; the bottom half is white with a blue/gray belt or band. The wings have white spots on them. Unlike most other birds, the kingfisher female has a different pattern than the male. Females have a second reddish-brown or rusty-orange band on their belly.

Did you know?

Skimmers get their name from how they feed; they skim the water with their mouth open, gliding through the water until they feel a fish in their mouth.

Nest Type

Most Active

Black Skimmer

Rynchops niger

Size: 15¾–19¾ inches long; wingspan of 43–45¼ inches; weighs 9¼–13 ounces

Habitat: Coastal sandy areas, lagoons, saltmarsh pools, beaches, islands, and sand bars

Range: They are year-round residents along the southeastern coastline; along the northern coastline, they are breeding residents. In North and South Carolina, they are year-round residents along the coast.

Food: Fish, shrimp, and molting crabs

Nesting: May to July

Nest: A scrape nest is dug that is 10 inches in diameter and 1 inch deep. They often nest with terns.

Eggs: 4–5 blue- or cream-colored eggs with black spots are laid per brood. Eggs are laid directly on the sand.

Young: Eggs hatch after a 22–25-day incubation. Chicks receive care from both parents. Within 14–17 days, the chicks start to learn to fly, and within 5 weeks, they will fledge. They will start to breed at around 2–4 years.

Predators: Pet cats, ghost crabs, gulls, crows, and raccoons

Migration: The population in the Carolinas are year-round residents but may migrate short distances.

Black skimmers are slender birds with a long beak and wings. They have a black-and-white feather pattern with black on top and white below. They have orange-red legs and an orange bill with a black tip. Juveniles are fluffier than adults and are brownish in color.

Did you know?

Turkey vultures have something most birds don't: a good sense of smell. Black vultures take advantage of this by soaring in circles above a turkey vulture and waiting until it finds food. Then they join in on the meal. A trick to tell them apart: Black vultures are all black with white wing tips. Turkey vultures make a black "T" shape when in flight and have light-gray undersides on their wings/tail.

Most Active

Black Vulture/Turkey Vulture

Coragyps atratus/Cathartes aura

Size: Black: 23½–27 inches long; wingspan is 53½–59 inches; weighs 3½–5 pounds. Turkey: 25¼–32 inches long; wingspan is 66–70 inches; weighs 4⅜ pounds

Habitat: Forests, woodland edges, cities, farmland

Range: Both species can be found throughout the southern US. Turkey vultures can be found in the northern US during the breeding season. Both can be found throughout the Carolinas year-round.

Food: Carrion (dead animals) like deer, snakes, feral hogs, coyotes, and armadillos. Black vultures may kill smaller animals if given the chance.

Nesting: Black: Caves, tree cavities, brush piles, abandoned buildings in large groups. Turkey: Secluded caves, cliff ledges, hollow trees, abandoned nests

Nest: Black: Existing cavities in nature. Turkey: A simple "scrape" nest of discarded plants or wood

Eggs: 1–3 speckled white eggs

Young: Black: Chicks fledge after 10 weeks but depend on their parents for several months. Turkey: Chicks fledge 70 days after hatching and are independent a week or so afterward.

Predators: Raccoons, opossums, and foxes prey on eggs. Snakes, eagles, hawks, and owls may attack juveniles or sick or injured adults. Healthy adults are rarely prey.

Migration: Vulture species do not migrate in the Carolinas.

Black vultures are all black with white wing tips. Turkey vultures look all black, but up close, they are different shades of light gray and brown. Turkey vultures have a red head.

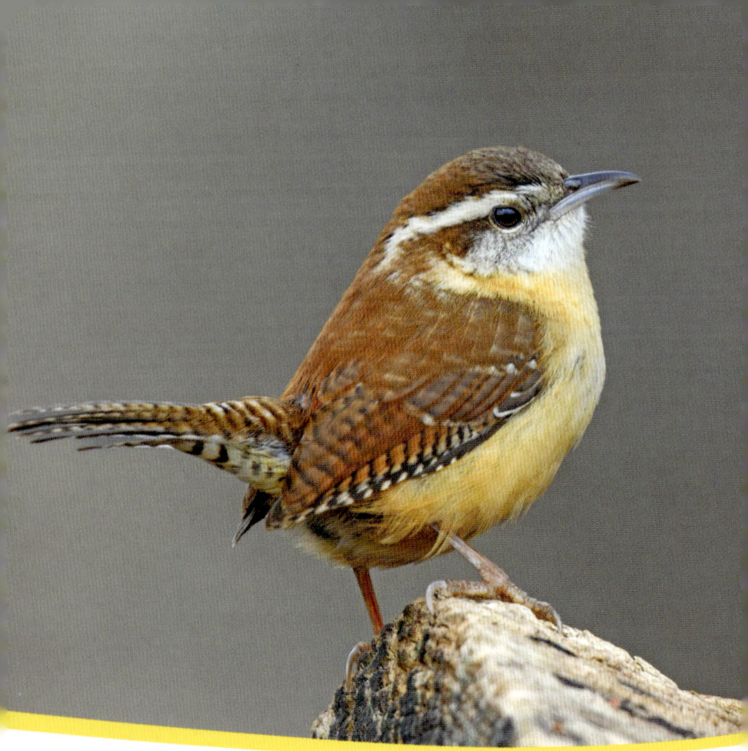

Did you know?

Only the male Carolina wren sings. They are the largest of the wren species found in North America.

Nest Type

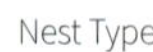

Most Active

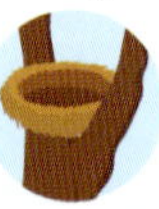

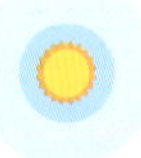

Carolina Wren

Thryothorus ludovicianus

Size: 4¾–5½ inches long; wingspan of 11½ inches; weighs ½–¾ ounce

Habitat: Fields, wooded areas with dense vegetation, suburban areas, overgrown farmlands, and shrubby areas

Range: They are found from eastern Canada to the coast of New England and as far south as Florida and Texas. They can be found statewide in North and South Carolina.

Food: Insects, seeds, fruit, spiders, lizards, frogs and sometimes snakes

Nesting: Mid-March to late September

Nest: They build a cup nest in open cavities in trees, as well as in human-made objects like wreaths and shoes. Nests are up to 9 inches long and 3 to 6 inches wide.

Eggs: 3–7 white, pinkish-white, or cream-colored eggs

Young: Chicks hatch 12–15 days after laying, covered in pale-gray down and with eyes closed. They will fledge from the nest within 10–16 days.

Predators: Snakes, pet cats, hawks, blue jays, foxes, raccoons, and squirrels

Migration: They do not migrate.

Both adult male and female look similar. They sport a reddish-brown top and buffy-orange-to-light-brown lower half. They have a white stripe near their brow, a white chin and throat, and a dark bill.

Did you know?

The double-crested cormorant does not have oil glands like other aquatic birds; this is why you will see it on a rock or a post with its wings spread: It's drying itself off. The cormorant's bill curves at the end, while the anhinga, a similar species that is often confused with a double-crested cormorant, has a pointed, straight-top bill.

Nest Type

Nest Type

Most Active

Migrates

Double-crested Cormorant

Nannopterum auritum

Size: 26–35 inches long; wingspan of 45–48½ inches; weighs 2½–3 pounds

Habitat: Freshwater lakes, rivers, swamps, coastal waters

Range: They can be found across North America. In the Carolinas, they can be found during migration in the interior areas of the states and as nonbreeding residents along the coastal areas.

Food: They are carnivores that eat fish, insects, snails, and crawfish.

Nesting: April to August; male chooses the nest site before finding a female. Nest in groups with other water birds

Nest: Veteran parents may repair an old nest. Otherwise, they build a new nest on the ground or in a tree. Nests are made of sticks and lined with grass.

Eggs: On average, 4 light-bluish-white eggs are laid at a time.

Young: Young chicks (shaglets) usually hatch in 25–28 days; they can swim immediately after hatching.

Predators: Eggs are vulnerable to raccoons, gulls, jays, foxes, and coyotes. Adults and chicks are preyed on by coyotes, foxes, raccoons, eagles, and great horned owls.

Migration: They migrate north to breed during the spring and overwinter in the Carolinas.

Adults have black feathers and topaz-colored eyes, with an orange bill, throat, and face area; they have black feet that are webbed like a duck's. The tail is short. During breeding season, adults may have a "double crest" of black feathers or sometimes white, depending on the location. This is where they get the name double-crested cormorant. Young are all brown or black.

Did you know?

Have you ever heard of a bird ordering someone to drink tea? Well, that's exactly what the eastern towhee does with its song of "DRINK your tea!"

Nest Type

Most Active

Eastern Towhee

Pipilo erythrophthalmus

Size: 7–8½ inches long; wingspan of 8–11 inches; weighs 1–2 ounces

Habitat: Open woodlands, forest edges, meadows, prairies, gardens, parks, and suburban areas

Range: They are found throughout the eastern US and southeast Canada. They are year-round residents in much of North Carolina, except in a small western area where they are breeding residents. In South Carolina, they are year-round residents statewide.

Food: Omnivores, they feed on seeds and fruits, as well as insects, snakes, lizards, and small amphibians.

Nesting: Nesting begins in spring and continues through the summer. The female constructs the nest.

Nest: Low in bushes or under shrubs on the ground. Nests are cup shaped and made out of woody plant material. The inside of the nest is lined with grasses.

Eggs: 2–6 eggs in a variety of colors, including cream, grayish pink, white, speckled brown, red, and purple

Young: Chicks are born blind and bald, except for a few areas with down feathers. Chicks receive food from both parents. Fledging takes place 10–12 days after hatching, but they will receive care for at least another month.

Predators: Snakes, hawks, and owls

Migration: Northern populations spend winter in the southern US. Year-round residents do not migrate.

Males have a dark-black head, tail, and upper body, while females are chocolate brown. Immature towhees are brown throughout. Both adults have burnt-orange or clay-colored sides and a white belly with white edges that run alongside the tail.

Did you know?

The eastern whip-poor-will gets its name from the call it makes, which sounds like it is saying, "whip-poor-will." They synchronize the laying of their eggs to match the phases of the lunar cycle. This allows them to time the hatching of their eggs to be around 10 days before the full moon.

Nest Type

Most Active

Migrates

Eastern Whip-poor-will

Antrostomus vociferus

Size: 8¾–10¼ inches long; wingspan of 17¾–19 inches; weighs 1½–2¼ ounces

Habitat: Forests that have open understories and scrubby woodlands

Range: They can be found across much of North America from mid-western Canada, eastward to Maine, as far south as Florida, and westward to Texas and Mexico. In the Carolinas, they can be found throughout both states as breeding residents and as winter residents in the lower Piedmont and Coastal Plain.

Food: They eat a variety of flying insects such as beetles.

Nesting: Late March to May

Nest: They lay eggs directly on the ground, often on leaf litter but also on bare ground, sand, or decaying wood.

Eggs: 2 grayish-white or cream-colored eggs

Young: Chicks hatch at around 20 days after laying. They are well developed at hatching, with tannish-orange-hued down and eyes closed. They start to explore outside the nest within a week.

Predators: Snakes, raccoons, skunks, coyotes, pet cats, foxes, and other birds will prey on the eggs.

Migration: Some will migrate to Central America to overwinter, while others migrate short distances.

Eastern whip-poor-wills have a rounded head, wide chest, and a brindled (mix of brown, gray, and tan) plumage that aids in camouflage or blending in to the bark of a tree. They have a long tail and wings. Males have white corners on their tail, while females have a dull buff-colored tail.

Did you know?

The golden-winged warbler weighs less than two nickels! The bird breeds with another warbler species (like blue-winged warblers) in a process called hybridization. Although it's cool that they can breed with other species, this, unfortunately, is one of the reasons that their population is in decline.

Nest Type

Most Active

Migrates

Golden-Winged Warbler

Vermivora chrysoptera

Size: 5 inches long; wingspan of 8 inches; weighs ¼–½ ounce

Habitat: Forests and forest edges, woodlands, old fields, scrublands, marshes, and orchards

Range: They are found from southern Canada to as far west as eastern Texas down through Central America into northern South America. They are found throughout a small sliver of western North Carolina during breeding season in the Appalachian Mountains.

Food: Caterpillars, moths and other insects, and spiders

Nesting: May to June

Nest: The cup-shaped nests are built on the ground by the female and usually hidden by vegetation.

Eggs: 3–6 pink or light-cream-colored eggs with streaks or small blotches are laid per brood.

Young: Eggs hatch 10–12 days after laying. Chicks are born with sparse feathers and will leave the nest (fledge) within 8 days.

Predators: American crows, eastern chipmunks, blue jays, and snakes

Migration: Migrate from South America to North America during the spring and return during fall migration

Golden-winged warblers are small songbirds with a slender body, short tail, and straight thin bill. The males have a black throat and ear patches with white borders around them. Males also have a golden crown and wing patch (hence the name). Females are similar to males but instead have lighter-gray patches on their ears and throat. Both sexes have white on their tails.

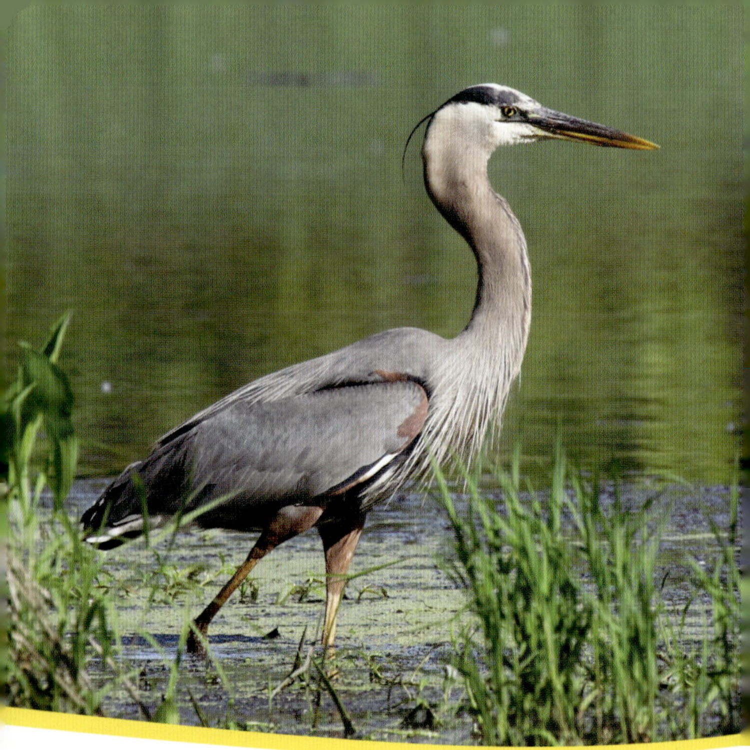

Did you know?
The great blue heron is the largest and most common heron species in North and South Carolina. A heron's eye color changes as it ages. The eyes start out gray but transition to yellow over time. Great blue herons swallow their prey whole.

Nest Type

Most Active

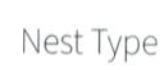

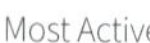

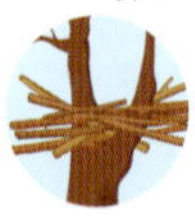

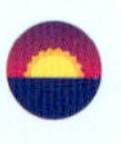

Great Blue Heron

Ardea herodias

Size: 3–4½ feet long; wingspan of 6–7 feet; weighs 5–7 pounds

Habitat: Lakes, ponds, rivers, marshes, lagoons, wetlands, and coastal areas like beaches

Range: They can be found throughout the United States and down into Mexico. In the Carolinas, they are found as year-round residents across both states.

Food: Fish, rats, crabs, shrimp, grasshoppers, crawfish, other birds, small mammals, snakes, and lizards

Nesting: May to August

Nest: 2–3 feet across and saucer shaped; often grouped in large rookeries (colonies) in tall trees along the water's edge. Nests are built out of sticks and are often located in dead trees more than 100 feet above the ground; nests are used year after year.

Eggs: 3–7 pale bluish eggs

Young: Chicks will hatch after 28 days of incubation; young will stay in the nest for around 10 weeks. They reach reproductive maturity at just under 2 years.

Predators: Eagles, crows, gulls, raccoons, bears, and hawks

Migration: In the Carolinas, they do not migrate.

The great blue heron is a large wading bird with blue and gray upper body feathers; the belly area is white. They have long yellow legs that they use to stalk prey in the water. Great blue herons are famous for stalking prey at the water's edge; their specially adapted feet keep them from sinking into the mud!

Did you know?

A great horned owl can exert a crushing force of over 300 pounds with its talons. Despite its name, the great horned owl doesn't have horns at all. Instead, the obvious tufts on its head are made of feathers. Scientists aren't sure exactly how the tufts function, but they may help them stay hidden.

Nest Type

Most Active

Great Horned Owl

Bubo virginianus

Size: Up to 23 inches long; wingspan of 45 inches; weighs 3 pounds

Habitat: Woods; swamps; desert edges; as well as heavily populated areas such as cities, suburbs, and parks

Range: They are found throughout the continent of North America. They are found statewide in both North and South Carolina as year-round residents.

Food: They eat a variety of foods, but mostly mammals. Sometimes they eat other birds as well.

Nesting: They have lifelong partnerships, with nesting season starting in early winter; egg-laying starts in mid-January to February.

Nest: Nests are found 20–50 feet off the ground. They tend to reuse nests from other raptors or hollowed-out trees.

Eggs: The female lays 2–4 whitish eggs. Eggs are incubated for around 30 days.

Young: Young can fly at around 9 weeks old. The parents care for and feed young for several months.

Predators: Young owls are preyed upon by foxes, coyotes, bears, and opossums. As adults, they are rarely attacked by other birds of prey, such as golden eagles and goshawks.

Migration: They do not migrate in the Carolinas.

They are bulky birds with large ear tufts, a rusty brown-to-grayish face with a black border, and large bright eyes. The body color tends to be brown; the wing pattern is checkered with an intermingled dark brown. The chest and belly areas are light brown and have white bars.

Did you know?

When viewed straight-on, the yellow portion on the mallard's bill resembles a cartoon dog's head. Most domesticated ducks share the mallard as their ancestor. Mallard feathers are waterproof; they use oil from the preen gland beneath their feathers to help aid in repelling water. Mallards are the most common duck in the United States and in North and South Carolina.

Nest Type

Most Active

Migrates

Mallard

Anas platyrhynchos

Size: 24 inches long; wingspan of 36 inches; weighs 2½–3 pounds

Habitat: Lakes, ponds, rivers, and marshes

Range: The population stretches across the United States and Canada into Mexico and as far north as central Alaska. They can be found statewide in South and North Carolina as year-round residents with other populations as nonbreeding residents.

Food: Insects, worms, snails, aquatic vegetation, sedge seeds, grasses, and wild rice

Nesting: April to August

Nest: The nest is constructed on the ground, usually near a body of water.

Eggs: 9–13 eggs

Young: Eggs hatch 26–28 days after being laid. The ducklings are fully feathered and have the ability to swim at the time of hatching. Ducklings are cared for until they're 2–3 months old and reach reproductive maturity at 1 year old.

Predators: Humans, crows, mink, coyotes, raccoons, and snapping turtles

Migration: Year-round and winter resident that migrates north to breed

Male mallards are gray with an iridescent green head with a tinge of purple spotting, a white line along the collar, rusty-brown chest, yellow bill, and orange legs and feet. Females are dull brown with a yellow bill, a bluish area near the tail, and orange feet.

Did you know?

They get their name from the whistling call they make, which some say sounds like "Bob White." Northern bobwhites are the only native quail in the eastern US. A group of quails is called a covey. Both male and female bobwhites perform courtship displays.

Nest Type

Most Active

Northern Bobwhite

Colinus virginianus

Size: 8–9¼ inches long; wingspan of 3½–4¾ inches; weighs 5–6 ounces

Habitat: Open areas such as prairies, farm fields, hedgerows, and grasslands, as well as pine forests

Range: Year-round residents in both North and South Carolina, they are widespread in eastern North America and southern Mexico.

Food: They eat mostly seeds and leaves. During the summer, they eat insects and spiders.

Nesting: June to August; the male and female choose a nesting site together.

Nest: Ground nest in the form of a scrape lined with dead vegetation and grass

Eggs: 7–28 creamy-to-dull-white eggs

Young: Chicks hatch at around 20–25 days after laying, covered in down feathers. They are able to move around within a few minutes to hours after hatching. Chicks are fed insects by both parents. They reach independence within a couple of weeks.

Predators: Hawks, owls, raccoons, opossums, skunks, foxes, and snakes

Migration: They are year-round residents.

Bobwhite quails are small ground birds with a round body. They have a short curved bill and a short tail. They are overall reddish brown with a dappling of white and brown mixed in that helps camouflage them. Males have a white throat and stripe above their brow that has a black border around it. Females on the other hand have a buffy-colored throat and brow.

Did you know?

Cardinals are very territorial. A cardinal will sometimes attack its own reflection, thinking that another cardinal has entered its territory. The early bird gets the worm, and cardinals are some of the first birds active in the morning.

Nest Type

Most Active

Northern Cardinal

Cardinalis cardinalis

Size: 8–9 inches long; wingspan of 12 inches

Habitat: Hardwood forests, urban areas, orchards, backyards, and fields

Range: They are found throughout eastern and midwestern parts of the United States with some populations extending as far west as Arizona. They are found statewide in North and South Carolina.

Food: Seeds, fruits, insects, spiders, and centipedes

Nesting: March to August

Nest: The cup-shaped nest is built by females in thick foliage, usually at least 1 foot off the ground. It can be 3 inches tall and 4 inches wide.

Eggs: The female lays 2–5 off-white eggs with a variety of colored speckles.

Young: About 2 weeks after eggs are laid, chicks hatch with their eyes closed and mostly naked, aside from sparsely placed down feathers.

Predators: Hawks, owls, and squirrels

Migration: Cardinals do not migrate.

Northern cardinal males are bright-red birds with a black face. Females are a washed-out red or brown. Both males and females have a crest (tuft of feathers on the head), an orange beak, and grayish legs. Cardinals can be identified by their laser-gun-like call.

Did you know?

Northern mockingbirds get their name from their ability to mimic or "mock" sounds of other birds, organisms, and even machines. They can sing 40 to more than 200 songs, depending on their region. Mockingbirds will bravely defend their nests from larger birds like raptors. When danger is present, mockingbirds can form an allegiance with neighbors to protect the shared area.

Most Active

Northern Mockingbird

Mimus polyglottos

Size: 8–10 inches long; wingspan of 12–14 inches; weighs 1½–2 ounces

Habitat: Hardwood forests, urban areas, parks, orchards, backyards, and fields

Range: They are found throughout the United States as permanent residents. They are year-round residents that are found statewide in North and South Carolina.

Food: Omnivore that feeds on seeds, fruits, insects, earthworms, and sometimes lizards

Nesting: Spring to early fall

Nest: The cup-shaped nest is built by both males and females, with the male doing most of the building. The nest is composed of twigs and lined on the inside with dead leaves, grass, moss, and manmade materials.

Eggs: 3–5 blue-to-green eggs speckled with brownish red

Young: About 2 weeks after the mother lays the eggs, chicks hatch. They're born nearly naked and with their eyes closed.

Predators: Pet cats, crows, snakes, blue jays, hawks, owls, and squirrels

Migration: Does not migrate

Mockingbirds are medium-size grayish songbirds. They have a white belly and dark-gray wings with a bold white patch. Mockingbirds have a long dark-gray tail with bright-white outer feathers.

Did you know?

The osprey is nicknamed the "fish hawk" because it is the only hawk in North America that mainly eats live fish. An osprey will rotate its catch to put it in line with its body, pointing headfirst, which allows for less resistance in flight as the air travels over the fish.

Nest Type

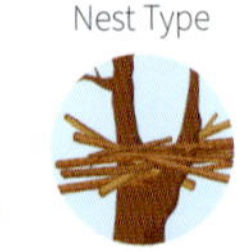

Most Active

Migrates

Osprey

Pandion haliaetus

Size: 21–23 inches long; wingspan of 59–71 inches; weighs 3–4½ pounds

Habitat: Near lakes, ponds, rivers, swamps, and reservoirs

Range: They are found throughout North America. In North Carolina, they are migrating visitors in the west, year-round residents on the coast, and breeding residents in the rest of the state. In South Carolina, they are breeding residents in the northern half of the state and year-round residents everywhere else.

Food: Mostly fish; sometimes mammals, birds, and reptiles

Nesting: For ospreys that migrate, egg-laying happens in April and May.

Nest: Platform nests are constructed out of twigs and sticks on trees or human-made objects.

Eggs: 1–3 cream-colored eggs with splotches of brown and pinkish red

Young: Chicks hatch after around 36 days and have brown-and-white down feathers. Ospreys fledge around 50–55 days after hatching and will receive care from parents for another 2 months or so.

Predators: Owls, eagles, foxes, skunks, raccoons, and snakes

Migration: Some migrate to breeding areas in the spring and return during the fall; others do not migrate.

Ospreys are raptors, and they have a brown upper body and white lower body. The wings are brown on the outside and white on the underside, with brown spotting and streaks toward the edge. The head is white with a brown band that goes through the eye area, highlighting the yellow eyes.

Did you know?

Painted buntings are the only birds in the United States that have a solid red breast and belly, and a solid blue head. Males do not get their iconic plumage until after their second year. Sometimes painted buntings will steal prey from spiders and their webs.

Nest Type

Most Active

Migrates

Painted Bunting

Passerina ciris

Size: 5½ inches long; wingspan of 8¾ inches; weighs ½ ounce

Habitat: Hardwood forests, urban areas, orchards, coastal areas, backyards, and fields

Range: They can be found in the US and the northern portion of Mexico as breeding residents and the southern portion of Mexico and Florida as nonbreeding residents. They are found along the coastal areas of both North and South Carolina as breeding residents.

Food: Omnivores; diet depends on the season. They feed on seeds, snails, insects, spiders, and caterpillars.

Nesting: March to early August. Males arrive first and pick a breeding area to defend. Both birds pick a nesting area.

Nest: The cup-shaped nest is built by females in thick foliage. The nest is woven out of leaves, bark, twigs, spiderwebs, and grasses. It is lined with grass and hair.

Eggs: 3–4 gray or blue-white eggs with brown or gray spots.

Young: Chicks hatch 12 days after eggs are laid; they are born mostly naked, with eyes closed. Both parents feed the young. The chicks fledge around day 12 but will receive care for at least 3 more weeks.

Predators: Hawks, owls, and squirrels

Migration: They migrate from southern Florida and Mexico in the spring and return to overwinter.

Male painted buntings are a brightly colored mix of blues, greens, reds, and yellows. Females and juveniles are dullish or semi-bright yellow to olive green with eye rings.

Did you know?

Purple gallinules can build up to four different nests in their lifetime. They build their nest on the water, anchoring it to nearby aquatic vegetation. They will sometimes move nestlings to a different nest. Their feet help to distribute their weight, allowing them to walk on vegetation.

Nest Type

Most Active

Migrates

Purple Gallinule

Porphyrio martinica

Size: 13–14½ inches long; wingspan of 21½–22 inches; weighs 7¼–10¼ ounces

Habitat: Freshwater swamps and marshes, ponds, freshwater coastal areas, lakes, and reservoirs

Range: They can be found along the coast of the southeastern US during the breeding season and year-round in southern Florida. They can be found in South Carolina as a breeding visitor.

Food: Seeds, fruits, flowers, insects, spiders, small fish, frogs, and eggs and chicks of other birds

Nesting: May to August

Nest: A cup-shaped nest is built in a marsh, sometimes on floating vegetation.

Eggs: 6–8 creamy-white eggs with brown spots

Young: Eggs hatch around 20 days after laying; chicks are born covered with black down and with eyes open. They are fed and incubated by both parents. The young use their wings for balance as they move around on lily pads until they can fly at around 9 weeks.

Predators: Alligators, turtles, snakes, raptors, foxes, and bobcats

Migration: They migrate to breeding grounds from Central America.

Purple gallinules display a variety of colors from red to blue and green. They get their name from the purple and indigo feathers on their head. They have long yellow legs and toes used for walking across the vegetation. Juveniles, duller than the adults, are mostly brown with highlights of their adult colors and darker legs.

Did you know?

The red-tailed hawk is the most abundant hawk in North America. (Look for it on power lines!) The red-tailed hawk's scream is the sound effect that you hear when soaring eagles are shown in movies. Eagles do not screech like hawks, so filmmakers use hawk calls instead!

Nest Type

Most Active

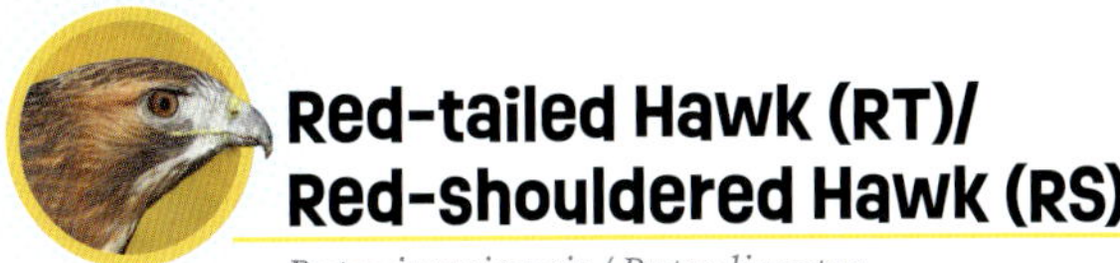

Red-tailed Hawk (RT)/ Red-shouldered Hawk (RS)

Buteo jamaicensis / Buteo lineatus

Size: RT: 19–25 inches long; wingspan of 47–57 inches; weighs 2½–4 pounds. RS: 16½–24 inches long; wingspan of 37–43 inches; weighs around 1 pound

Habitat: RT: Deserts, woodlands, fields. RS: Forests, swamps, grasslands, urban areas

Range: RT: Throughout North America; in the Carolinas, they are found across the states as year-round residents. RS: Throughout eastern North America; in the Carolinas, they are found throughout as year-round residents.

Food: RT: Rodents, birds, reptiles, bats, and insects. RS: Small mammals, lizards, snakes, crawfish, songbirds

Nesting: Hawks mate for life; nesting starts in March.

Nest: RT: Both parents build a large cup-shaped nest (can be 6 feet high and 3 feet wide), made of sticks and branches. RS: Both male and female build a cup-shaped nest 20 feet off the ground.

Eggs: RT: White with colored blotches. RS: Off-white or slightly blue with varied markings

Young: RT: Young hatch after 30 days. They can fly at 5–6 weeks. RS: Chicks can fly after 5–6 weeks.

Predators: RT: Owls and crows. RS: Snakes, mammals, and owls

Migration: Does not migrate

Red-tailed hawks are named for their rusty-red tails! They have brown heads and a creamy, light-brown chest with a band of brown streaking. Red-shouldered hawks have a reddish-brown head and back, with rusty undersides with white barring across the belly.

Did you know?

The sandhill crane is the most abundant crane species in the world. They are not afraid to defend themselves when threatened. They will use their feet and bill to ward off predators, often stabbing attackers with their bill. Sometimes sandhill cranes will travel 500 miles in one day to find food.

Nest Type

Most Active

Migrates

Sandhill Crane

Grus canadensis

Size: 3½–4 feet long; wingspan of 6–7 feet; weighs 7½–10 pounds

Habitat: Grasslands, savannas, and farm fields

Range: They can be found across North America in various parts of the year. They overwinter in California, Mexico, Texas, and Florida and breed in Canada, Oregon, Washington state, Minnesota, and other states across the northern Midwest and New England area. They can be found in the Carolinas during migration.

Food: Berries, insects, snails, amphibians, and small mammals, as well as food crops like corn

Nesting: Nonmigratory populations will lay eggs from December to August, while populations that migrate will nest between April and May.

Nest: Both adults build the cup-shaped nest using vegetation from nearby areas.

Eggs: Up to 3 pale brownish-yellow eggs with brown spots

Young: Chicks are born with the ability to see and walk. Chicks become independent at around 9 months and will start breeding between 2 and 7 years.

Predators: Coyotes, raccoons, ravens, great horned owls, and humans

Migration: Some populations use the Carolinas as a pitstop during migration.

The sandhill crane is a large bird with gray-to-brownish feathers with a white face and ruby-red crown. They are commonly seen in large groups in fields.

Did you know?

White ibises will wash their food before eating itt. When they find an item that is very muddy, they will dunk it in the water before consuming it. White ibises are very social birds that live and nest in groups or colonies. Often other wading birds, like egrets, will follow behind them when they are foraging because they will stir up food that the egrets eat.

Nest Type

Most Active

Migrates

White Ibis

Eudocimus albus

Size: 22–24 inches tall; wingspan of 3 feet; weighs 3 pounds

Habitat: Marshes, swamps, mud flats, mangroves, coastal and estuarine areas, ponds, and flooded fields

Range: White ibises can be found along the Atlantic and Gulf coasts of the US. They are found in the coastal areas of eastern NC during migration and along the coast as year-round residents. In SC, they are found from the Piedmont region to the coast during migration and year-round along the coast.

Food: Carnivores that mostly feed on crawfish, crabs, insects, frogs, lizards, snails, and small fish

Nesting: Takes place in the spring when the female selects the site near water and usually in a shrub or tree branches. Nesting happens in colonies with other wading birds. Both parents provide care to chicks.

Nest: Both adults build a messy platform using vegetation. The nest is about 10 inches wide and 2–4 inches tall.

Eggs: 1–5 creamy to bluish-green eggs with brown spots

Young: Chicks hatch 3 weeks after laying, with eyes closed and covered in down feathers. They fledge at around 28 days and become independent at around 7 weeks.

Predators: Crows, raccoons, alligators, snakes, black-crowned night herons, opossums, owls, and humans

Migration: Some will migrate to the Carolinas during the spring and migrate north during fall.

White ibises are mostly white, except for the black tips of the wings. They have a long reddish-pink bill and legs. The skin around their blue eyes is also pink. Immatures are a marbled brown and white with a paler bill and legs.

Did you know?

Turkeys sometimes fly at night, unlike most birds, and land in trees to roost. Turkeys have some interesting facial features; the red skin growth on a turkey's face above the beak is called a snood, while the growth under the beak is called a wattle. Wild turkeys can have more than 5,000 feathers.

Nest Type

Most Active

Wild Turkey

Meleagris gallopavo

Size: 3–4 feet long; wingspan of 5 feet; males weigh 16–25 pounds; females weigh 9–11 pounds.

Habitat: Woodlands and grasslands

Range: They can be found in the eastern US and have been introduced in many western areas of the country. They are year-round residents statewide in both North and South Carolina.

Food: Grain, snakes, frogs, insects, acorns, berries, and ferns

Nesting: April to September

Nest: The nest is built on the ground using leaves as bedding, in brush or near the base of trees or fallen logs.

Eggs: 10–12 tan eggs with very small reddish-brown spots

Young: Poults (young) hatch about a month after eggs are laid; they will flock with the mother for a year. When young are still unable to fly, the mom will stay on the ground with her poults to provide protection and warmth. When poults grow up, they are known as hens if they are female, or as gobblers or toms if they are male.

Predators: Humans, foxes, raccoons, owls, eagles, skunks

Migration: Turkeys do not migrate.

A wild turkey is a large bird that is dark brown and black with some iridescent feathers. Males will fan out their tail to attract a mate. When threatened, they will also fan out their tail and rush the predator, sometimes kicking and puncturing prey with the spurs on their feet.

Did you know?

Wood storks are the only species of storks that breed in the US. Wood storks will sometimes steal the nest of another wood stork, throwing the eggs and young out of the nest. While their legs are actually black, oftentimes they look white because they will use the restroom on themselves as a way to keep cool. The white color comes from a chemical called uric acid, which turns into a white paste mixed in with their waste.

Nest Type

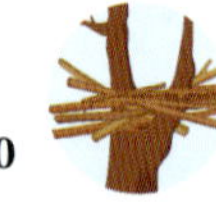

Most Active

Migrates

Wood Stork

Mycteria americana

Size: 33½–45½ inches tall; wingspan of 60–65 inches; weighs about 4–6 pounds

Habitat: Freshwater marshes, mangroves, flooded fields, ponds, lakes, lagoons, streams, swamps, and rivers

Range: Breeding populations are in Florida, Georgia, Alabama, and the Carolinas. In NC, they are found in the eastern coastal area as wintering residents and as breeding residents in the easternmost portion. They are found in SC from the Piedmont to the coast as wintering residents, and as breeding residents along the coast.

Food: Fish, rodents, crawfish, turtles, crabs, aquatic insects, snakes, baby alligators, frogs, and plants

Nesting: March to August, they nest colonially in trees.

Nest: Platform nest is built by both male and female using twigs and sticks. The inside is lined with leaves.

Eggs: Female lays one clutch of 3–5 creamy-white eggs.

Young: Eggs hatch about a month after being laid. Chicks will leave the nest after a day and fly within 8 weeks. Fledging takes place 2 months after hatching. They reach reproductive age at around 4 years.

Predators: Raccoons, skunks, fish, snapping turtles, alligators, humans, snakes, and other wood storks

Migration: They migrate to and from Florida to breed in the Carolinas.

The wood stork is a large white bird with a bare head and neck of slate gray. Wings and tail are iridescent black to green. Feet, bill, and legs are black, and the toes are pink during breeding season. Immatures have a feathered head and yellow-gray bill.

Did you know?

The male alligator does not have vocal cords. The growling or roaring sound that males make in order to attract females comes from the alligator filling its lungs with air and exhaling. Alligators sometimes trick birds into landing or flying close to them by placing sticks and vegetation on their head; birds looking for nesting material will fly and try to retrieve the sticks and be met by the gator's mouth.

Most Active

American Alligator

Alligator mississippiensis

Size: 8–16 feet long; weighs up to 1,000 pounds

Habitat: Freshwater ponds, coastal areas, rivers, swamps, and brackish water (mix of fresh and saltwater)

Range: They are native to the southeastern United States from Florida to North Carolina and as far west as Texas.

Food: Opportunistic carnivores that feed on snakes, fish, birds, mammals, insects, and sometimes even fruit

Mating: Starts in spring and goes until May or early June. Mating takes place at night. Males have multiple mates.

Nest: Nests are made of plant material and can be 3 feet tall by 7 feet wide. Eggs are covered with vegetation.

Eggs: 35–50 white eggs

Young: Eggs hatch about 2 months after laying. Hatchling sex is temperature dependent; nest temperatures below 88 degrees or above 90½ degrees usually produce females, and temperatures of 89½ to around 90½ degrees usually produce males. They reach independence at 1 year and reproductive age at around 10 years. Hatchlings form pods or groups and alert others to nearby danger by making clicking noises.

Predators: Humans; as juveniles: birds, snakes, bobcats, raccoons, otters, large fish, and older alligators

The American alligator is a thick-bodied reptile with short legs. It has a wide U-shaped snout. The body has thick skin in colors of black to brownish gray; the tail is thick and muscular, and the underside is white. Hatchlings are striped for the first several months. If the water freezes, alligators will bury themselves in mud and stick their snouts out for several days.

Did you know?

The snapping turtle's sex is determined by the temperature of the nest! Nest temperatures that are 67–68 degrees produce females, temperatures in the range between 70 and 72 degrees produce both males and females, and nests that are 73–75 degrees will usually produce all males.

Most Active

Hibernates

Common Snapping Turtle

Chelydra serpentina

Size: 8–16 inches long; weighs 10–35 pounds

Habitat: Rivers, marshes, and lakes; can be found in areas that have brackish water (freshwater and saltwater mixture)

Range: They are found throughout North and South Carolina; also found in the eastern US and southern Canada.

Food: These omnivores (eaters of both plants and animals) eat frogs, reptiles, snakes, birds, small mammals, and plants.

Mating: April to November are the breeding months; lays eggs during June and July.

Nest: Females dig a hole in sandy soil and lay the eggs into it.

Eggs: 25–42 eggs, sometimes as many as 80 or more

Young: Like sea turtles, snapping turtles have temperature-dependent sex determination (TSD), meaning the temperature of the nest determines the sex of the young. Hatchlings leave the nest between August and October. In the North, turtles mature at around 15–20 years, while southern turtles mature around 12 years old.

Predators: Raccoons, skunks, crows, dogs, and humans

The snapping turtle's carapace (top shell) is dark green to brown and usually covered in algae or moss. The plastron (or bottom of the shell) is smaller than the carapace. They are crepuscular animals that are mostly active during the dawn and dusk hours. Young turtles will actively look for food. As adults, they rely heavily on ambushing to hunt; they bury themselves in the sand with just the tip of their nose and eyes showing.

Did you know?

Terrapins live in brackish water (mix of salt and freshwater). They have special glands called lachrymal salt glands that help them get rid of salt in the body. Terrapins have powerful jaws that help them in eating different types of animals with shells, like snails and clams. Diamondback terrapins get their name from the diamond-shaped markings on their carapace (top shell).

Most Active

Hibernates

Diamondback Terrapin

Malaclemys terrapin

Size: Male: 5½–6 inches long; weighs ½ pound. Female: 11–12 inches long; weighs 1½ pounds

Habitat: Coastal areas like estuaries, tidal creeks, salt marshes, mangroves, and lagoons

Range: They can be found as far north as Massachusetts and as far south as the Florida Keys, and westward into Texas. They can be found along the coast of both North and South Carolina.

Food: Fish, crabs, mussels, marine snails, insects, carrion (dead things), clams, and other mollusks

Mating: May to June

Nest: Nests are usually in sand dunes or scrub vegetation.

Eggs: Female will lay 2 or 3 clutches a year. Clutches range from 4–23 eggs, but usually 5–10 pinkish-white eggs.

Young: Hatchlings usually emerge 2–3 months after laying and are fully independent at hatching. Like other turtles, terrapins have temperature-dependent sex determination. Females mature around year 7, but due to their smaller size, males mature around 2 or 3 years.

Predators: Wild hogs, herons, raccoons, humans, crabs, rats, gulls, crows, mink, and foxes

The diamondback terrapin is a species of turtle native to the eastern and southern United States and Bermuda. The shell appears wedge-shaped and can vary from brown to gray. The body can be gray, brown, yellow, or white. All have a unique pattern of wiggly, black markings or spots on their body and head. Diamondback terrapins have large, webbed feet and are very strong swimmers.

Did you know?

Eastern box turtles help to spread various species of plants. As omnivores, they will eat different types of berries, and as they move to other locations, they expel the seeds in their waste, creating new plants when those seeds grow. They have the ability to bring their limbs and head under their shell and shut themselves inside.

Most Active

Hibernates

Eastern Box Turtle

Terrapene carolina carolina

Size: 5–6 inches long; weighs 5–5½ ounces

Habitat: Forests, open grasslands, pastures, shrublands, wetlands, farm fields

Range: Can be found as far north as Maine, as far south as Florida, and as far west as Texas. They can be found statewide in both North and South Carolina.

Food: They are omnivores that eat earthworms, slugs, grasses, berries, mushrooms, and carrion.

Mating: Late spring to early autumn

Nest: Shallow nest built in loose material (dirt, soil, sandy clay)

Eggs: 1–9 eggs

Young: Hatchlings hatch 50–70 days after laying and will reach reproductive maturity at around 5 years old.

Predators: Crows, ravens, hawks, owls, raccoons, foxes, and squirrels

Eastern box turtles have sharp beaks, thick limbs, and a dome-shaped carapace (top of shell). The carapace is brownish to black and has various patterns of orange and yellowish spots. The skin is dark brown to yellowish tan with orange, yellow, and red spots. Males have bluish spots on their cheeks, legs, and throat. Males also have red irises, while the females have brown.

Did you know?

Copperheads get their name from their copper- to bronze-colored head. A copperhead's size can give a hint to how large its fangs are. The larger or longer the snake, the longer the fangs usually are. Young copperheads are born with a bright-yellow tail that aids the young snake in catching prey. The snake moves its tail around like a worm to lure would-be prey.

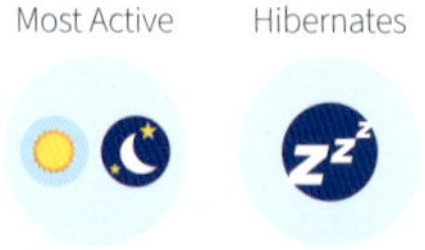

Most Active

Hibernates

Safety Note: This snake is venomous (toxic). If you see one, observe or admire it from a distance.

Eastern Copperhead

Agkistrodon contortrix

Size: 22–40 inches long; weighs 4–10 ounces or larger

Habitat: Dry rocky hillsides, lowland forest areas, grasslands, water-adjacent wooded areas, and suburban areas

Range: They live throughout the eastern and central US. They can be found throughout North and South Carolina.

Food: Carnivore. Adults eat mostly rodents like mice and rats but also baby cottontails, small birds, swamp rabbits, lizards, baby turtles, small snakes, amphibians, and insects (especially cicadas and grasshoppers).

Mating: April to May and late August to October. Males produce a pheromone that makes the female unattractive to other males.

Nest: Copperheads do not make nests but utilize natural dens or dens made by other animals. Dens are often near water sources, in rock crevices, hollowed-out logs or downed trees, or in shrub piles.

Eggs: Copperheads are ovoviviparous: the eggs develop in the body, and the mother then gives live birth.

Young: Females give live birth to 5–8 (sometimes as many as 20) 6–10-inch-long young. These snakes reach sexual maturity at 4 years. They are independent at birth.

Predators: Snakes, raptors, raccoons, and opossums

Copperheads have a triangular or arrow-like, copper-bronze head. Eyes have vertical tear-shaped pupils. The thick body comes in varieties of tans, browns, dirty oranges, and copper. They have 10–18 hourglass-shaped bands. Copperheads are the only species with this hourglass shape. Juveniles have the same pattern but fewer hourglass shapes. They also have a yellow-tipped tail that fades away by age 3 or 4.

Did you know?

The eastern coral snake is venomous, even though it does not have an arrow-shaped head. This proves that what's true for some venomous snakes is not true for all venomous snakes. Western coral snakes are the only snakes in the eastern part of the US that have fangs fixed in the front of their mouth.

Most Active

Hibernates

Safety Note: This snake is venomous (toxic). If you see one, observe or admire it from a distance.

Eastern Coral Snake

Micrurus fulvius

Size: 18–30 inches long (rarely over 17 inches); weight ranges widely

Habitat: Grasslands, suburban areas, flatwoods and scrub areas, woodlands, forests, wetlands and the borders of swamps, and coastal plain areas like sandhills

Range: They can be found from North Carolina through Florida and the southern parts of Georgia into the southeastern areas of Louisiana. They are found in the southeastern portions of North and South Carolina.

Food: Frogs, snakes, lizards, insects, and sometimes mammals

Mating: Late spring to early fall

Nest: No nest; they will use natural cavities in the ground or abandoned burrows of small mammals. The eggs are often laid underground or in leaf litter.

Eggs: 4–12 white, leathery eggs that are elongated

Young: Snakelets hatch around 2 months after laying. They are around 7–9 inches at hatching. No parental care is given. Females become mature around 21 months and males become mature around 11–21 months.

Predators: Snakes, raptors like American kestrels and hawks, bullfrogs, loggerhead shrikes, and cats. Eggs and juveniles are vulnerable to red ants.

Eastern coral snakes have a striped body with a pattern of red, black, and yellow bands or rings. The red and yellow touch, followed by the black. The nose is black with the rest of the head being yellow. The red stripes have black specks within them. Juveniles have a similar pattern as the adults but brighter in color. The pattern darkens as the snake ages.

Did you know?

Eastern garter snakes are highly social and will form groups with other snakes and often other species to overwinter together in a burrow or hole. When threatened by a predator or handled, they will sometimes musk or emit a foul-smelling, oily substance from their cloaca (butt).

Most Active

Hibernates

Eastern Garter Snake

Thamnophis sirtalis

Size: 14–36 inches long (rarely over 17 inches); weighs 5–5½ ounces

Habitat: Forests and forest edges, grasslands, and suburban areas

Range: They can be found in the US from Minnesota, southward to eastern Texas, and then east towards the Atlantic Coast. They can be found statewide in both North and South Carolina.

Food: Frogs, snails, toads, salamanders, insects, fish, and worms

Mating: April or May

Nest: No nest; they will use natural cavities in the ground or abandoned burrows of small mammals.

Eggs: No eggs are laid. Eastern garter snakes are born live in a litter of 8–20 snakes.

Young: Snakelets are 4½–9 inches long at birth; no parental care is given.

Predators: Crows, ravens, hawks, owls, raccoons, foxes, and squirrels

Eastern garter snakes are black with three yellow stripes running down their body on the back and sides. They withstand winter by gathering in groups inside the burrows of rodents or under human-made structures, and they enter brumation, or a state of slowed body activity.

Did you know?

The eastern glass lizard is not a snake, though it lacks legs and therefore looks like one. A few characteristics that let us know that it is a lizard are that it has eyelids that move (snakes do not have eyelids) and its tail is as long, or longer, than its body. Eastern glass lizards get their name from how their tails detach when they are scared or captured. The detached tail separates from the body, making it look like the lizard has shattered into pieces.

Most Active

Hibernates

Eastern Glass Lizard

Ophisaurus ventralis

Size: 18–42½ inches long; weighs 11–21 ounces

Habitat: Coastal plains, forests, savannas, shrubland wetlands, wet meadows, maritime forests, grasslands, damp grassy areas, and sandy environments such as dunes

Range: Their range spans from southern Florida up through Georgia into North Carolina and as far west as Louisiana. They can be found in both North and South Carolina from the central portions of the states eastward towards the coastal area.

Food: Carnivores that feed on a variety of prey such as small mice, grasshoppers, spiders, snails, beetles, and the eggs of reptiles and birds

Mating: Late spring through the end of summer

Nest: Nests are usually depressions in sandy soil or under natural covering. The female will guard the eggs until they hatch.

Eggs: 5–15 eggs are laid in June and July.

Young: Young are born in August and September. They are 7 inches long, khaki to beige, with dark stripes along the side. The young are independent at hatching.

Predators: Hawks, raccoons, foxes, coyotes, bobcats, skunks, and other mammals. Several snake species also feed on glass lizards.

Eastern glass lizards are black with greenish-yellow-to-tan markings trailing down their body from their nose down to their tail. The nose and underside are various shades of tans and yellows. Juveniles are khaki or beige to brown in color overall with black streak markings going down both sides.

Did you know?

The eastern hognose snake is venomous! But its venom is not harmful to us. The hognose's teeth have a dual purpose: They inject venom into prey and also deflate toads who puff their bodies up to avoid being eaten. The hognose wards off would-be predators by flattening its head to look like a cobra. If that doesn't work, it will play dead by flipping its body over and letting its tongue hang out of its mouth.

Most Active 

Hibernates 

Eastern Hognose Snake

Heterodon platirhinos

Size: 2–2½ feet long; weighs 2–4 ounces

Habitat: Shrublands, prairies, grasslands, coastal areas, and forests

Range: In the United States it has an expansive range southward into Florida and westward into Texas and parts of Kansas. They can be found statewide in both North and South Carolina.

Food: Frogs, toads, salamanders, birds, and invertebrates

Mating: April and May

Nest: Eastern hognose snakes dig burrows and will lay eggs under rocks, leaves, or in rotting logs.

Eggs: In June to July they will dig a burrow and lay 8–40 eggs (average clutch is around 25).

Young: 60 days after being laid, the eggs hatch. They do not receive care from parents at birth. Snakes reach full maturity around 20 months.

Predators: Hawks, snakes, raccoons, and opossums

The eastern hognose is a thick-bodied snake that gets its name from its shovel-like snout that it uses to dig in soil. They come in a variety of colors from red and brown to gray and black; they even come in versions of orange and red. Their underbody is lighter than their top.

Did you know?

King snakes get their name because they eat a variety of different snake species, many of which are venomous. It's a good thing king snakes have a resistance to venom. Eastern king snakes will mimic rattlesnakes when disturbed, vibrating their tails.

Most Active

Hibernates

Eastern King Snake

Lampropeltis getula

Size: 36–48 inches long; weighs 4–5 pounds

Habitat: Hardwood forests, swamps, pine forest, fields, freshwater marshes, and city areas

Range: They can be found in southern New Jersey to northern Florida, west to the Appalachians. They are found throughout South Carolina and most of North Carolina, except for the northwestern areas that border Tennessee and Virginia.

Food: Rodents, birds, snakes, lizards, and turtle eggs

Mating: March to May

Nest: Nests are usually in abandoned burrows, under a log, or made in moist soil.

Eggs: 4–20 white eggs

Young: HHatchlings emerge 60 days after eggs are laid; the young are brightly colored, weigh around 9–14 grams, and are approximately 5–8 inches long. Females become reproductively mature around 2–3 years and males around 1–2 years.

Predators: Raccoons, snakes, hawks, alligators, skunks, and opossums

The eastern king snake is a thick black snake with small eyes. Scales are smooth. It has white-to-yellow bands across the back. Snakes from mountainous areas usually have thinner bands or are almost completely black, and snakes from the coastal plain have wider bands.

Did you know?

The eastern tiger salamander can grow up to 13 inches long and live over 20 years! Eastern tiger salamanders migrate to their birthplace in order to breed, sometimes over a mile or more. Eastern tiger salamanders have a hidden weapon! They produce a poisonous toxin that is secreted or released from two glands in their tail. This toxin makes them taste bad to predators and allows them to escape.

Most Active

Hibernates

Eastern Tiger Salamander

Ambystoma tigrinum

Size: 7–13 inches long; weighs 4½ ounces

Habitat: Woodlands, marshes, and meadows; they spend most of their time underground in burrows.

Range: They are mostly found in the eastern US, with a smaller population introduced in the West. They can be found nearly statewide in South Carolina and in the eastern portion of North Carolina.

Food: Carnivores (eaters of meat), they eat insects, frogs, worms, and snails.

Mating: Tiger salamanders leave their burrows to find standing bodies of freshwater. They breed in late winter and early spring after the ground has thawed.

Nest: No nest, but eggs are joined together into one group in a jelly-like sack called an egg mass. An egg mass is attached to plant material at the bottom of a pond.

Eggs: There are 20–100 eggs or more in an egg mass.

Young: Eggs hatch after 2 weeks, and the young are fully aquatic with external gills. Limbs develop shortly after hatching; within 3 months, the young are fully grown but will hang around in a vernal pool. Individuals living in permanent ponds can take up to 6 months to fully develop.

Predators: Young are preyed upon by diving beetles, fish, turtles, and herons. Adults are preyed upon by snakes, owls, and badgers.

Eastern tiger salamanders have thick black, brown, or grayish bodies with uneven spots of yellow, tan, brown, or green along the head and body. The underside is usually a variation of yellow. Males are usually larger and thicker than females.

Did you know?

Gopher tortoises are keystone species, meaning that other animals depend on them for their survival. Over 350 species of animals depend on or benefit from the burrows that gopher tortoises make. These burrows are on average 15 feet long and over 6 feet deep. Some tortoises make burrows that are over 30 feet long and 10 feet deep. The gopher tortoise is the only native species of tortoise that can be found east of the Mississippi River.

Most Active

Hibernates

Gopher Tortoise

Gopherus polyphemus

Size: 9–15 inches long; weighs 10–13 pounds

Habitat: Longleaf pine sandhills, scrub, pine flatwoods, coastal grasslands, dunes, and prairies

Range: Gopher tortoises can be found in the coastal plain area of the United States from the most southern areas of South Carolina, south through Georgia and Florida, and westward to eastern Louisiana.

Food: Herbivores (plant eaters) that feed on grasses, fruits, and flowers. Sometimes they will eat carrion (dead things).

Mating: March to October

Nest: Usually occurs in areas that are bare and receive a lot of sun. Oftentimes there is a mounded area in front of the burrow, also known as the burrow apron.

Eggs: 5–9 white, sphere-shaped, Ping-Pong-ball-size eggs

Young: Hatchlings emerge about 2 inches long 90–110 days after laying. They are independent at the time of hatching. Males reach adulthood in around 9–12 years and females around 10–21 years.

Predators: Eagles, raccoons, bears, hawks, foxes, coyotes, bobcats, armadillos, fire ants, skunks, and dogs

Gopher tortoises have a smushed dome-shaped carapace that is somewhat flattened and comes in shades of brown and gray. Skin is scaly and can be shades of gray to tan and brown. They have forelimbs that are flat and aid in digging. Juveniles have yellow-hued skin and scutes (hard plates on the shell) that are yellow in the center and get darker with age.

Did you know?

The green anole is the only species of anole that is native to the United States. The male does pushups to attract a mate and defend its territory. They will extend the dewlap (a skin fold under the chin) and bob their head up and down in the presence of a rival male. Green anoles can change colors! Although not as elaborate as chameleons, they can change to various shades of green and brown.

Most Active

Hibernates

Green Anole

Anolis carolinensis

Size: 5–8 inches long; weighs 1–6 grams, the same as a penny or two

Habitat: Moist forests, coastal areas, shrublands, urban areas, swamps, and farmlands

Range: Anoles are found throughout North Carolina, South Carolina, Georgia, and Florida, as well as the Gulf Coast states of Alabama, Mississippi, Louisiana, and Texas.

Food: Carnivore that feeds on insects and other soft-bodied animals like spiders, flies, crickets, and grasshoppers.

Mating: April to September, males will patrol a territory and defend it from other males. Males attract females by extending their dewlap (pink-colored skin under chin) and bobbing up and down.

Nest: Shallow depression in soft soil, leaf litter, compost, rotting wood, or even a hole in a nearby tree

Eggs: 1–10 soft-shelled eggs are laid 2 to 4 weeks after mating.

Young: Hatching takes place 30–45 days after laying. Anoles are 2–2½ inches at hatching and are fully independent.

Predators: Lizards, birds, cats, dogs, frogs, and snakes

Green anoles come in many shades of greens and browns. What color you see depends on their surroundings and the condition that they are in. Males have a bright-red-to-ruby-pink skinfold or dewlap that extends under the chin. This dewlap serves a dual purpose of finding mates and deterring rival males from entering its territory. The female dewlap is much smaller and comes in shades of pink to almost white. Females have a white stripe that runs along their back.

Did you know?

Loggerheads get their odd name because sailors originally mistook them for logs or tree trunks. Unlike other sea turtles, green sea turtles are mostly herbivores (plant eaters). They eat algae and other plants, which gives their fat and muscles a greenish tint, leading to their name!

Most Active

Loggerhead Sea Turtle (LST)/ Green Sea Turtle (GST)

Caretta caretta / Chelonia mydas

Size: LST: 2½–3½ feet long; weighs 200–375 pounds. GST: 3–4½ feet long; weighs 250–500 pounds

Habitat: Coastal areas and open ocean

Range: They are found around the world where the water is warm enough, including off the coasts of North and South Carolina.

Food: LST: Crabs, jellyfish, conches, fish. GST: Seagrass and algae

Mating: (LST) May to August and (GST) June to September. Mating takes place every 2–4 years.

Nest: LST: A cavity around 18 inches deep. GST: A cavity about 30 inches deep. Both species nest above the surf line (where waves crash) on beaches. Females can lay multiple batches of eggs a season and usually will lay a new nest after about 14 days or so.

Eggs: LST: 100–130 eggs. GST: 100–130 Ping-Pong-ball-size eggs

Young: After 2 months of incubating, hatchlings emerge and immediately travel toward the ocean.

Predators: Feral hogs, sharks, raccoons, dogs, humans, crows, birds, fish, ants, crabs, cats, coyotes, foxes, bears, and skunks

Loggerheads have a distinctive large head and heart-shaped carapace (shell) that ranges from brown to red. The underside is paler and yellow to off-white. Green sea turtles are the second-largest sea turtle (the leatherback is bigger). Their shell is dark brown to olive colored with a yellow-to-pale plastron (underside).

Did you know?
Northern watersnakes are one of the most common watersnakes in the US. When they bite, they release a type of chemical substance called an anticoagulant, which prevents the blood from clotting, making whatever they bite bleed a lot. Their bite is not deadly to humans; however, it is still a good idea to keep your distance.

Most Active

Hibernates

Northern Watersnake

Nerodia sipedon

Size: 2¼–4½ feet long; weighs 5½–14½ ounces (females) and 3–5½ ounces (males)

Habitat: Near riverbanks and lakes

Range: They can be found across the eastern portion of North America, from southern Canada, as far south as Florida, westward to Texas, and as far east as Maine. In South Carolina, they are found mostly in the eastern portion of the state from the Piedmont region northward. In North Carolina, they are found throughout most of the state.

Food: Fish, amphibians such as frogs, smaller or baby reptiles, rodents, small mammals, and invertebrates

Mating: April–June

Nest: They do not create nests but use rock crevices and old dens and borrows to give live birth, as well as for shelter and to bask.

Eggs: No eggs are laid; they give birth to live young.

Young: After a 3–5-month pregnancy, 12–36 live young are born at a time. They are fully independent at birth, and reproductively mature at around 21 months for males and 36 months for females.

Predators: Raccoons, herons, skunks, foxes, larger snakes, pet cats, hawks, and egrets

Northern watersnakes are medium- to large-bodied snakes that come in various shades of brown, tan, grayish, and buffy color with a pale cream, yellow, or gray underside. They have dark blotches that run down their back. Sometimes they are confused with the nonvenomous banded watersnake, as well as the venomous cottonmouth. Young are lighter than adults.

Did you know?

When threatened, a rattlesnake shakes its rattle to warn would-be predators. These snakes are all venomous (their bites inject venom, a toxin), so do not go near one or try to pick one up! Instead, leave it alone, so it can help people by munching on rodents and other pests! Rattlesnakes are "pit vipers," snakes that have a special body part that helps them "see" heat.

Most Active

Hibernates

Safety Note: These snakes are venomous (toxic). If you see one, observe or admire them from a distance.

Rattlesnakes

Eastern Diamondback Rattlesnake (EDR) (*Crotalus adamanteus*), Timber Rattlesnake (TR) (*Crotalus horridus*), Pygmy Rattlesnake (PR) (*Sistrurus miliarius*)

Size: EDR: 33–72 inches long; weighs 10 pounds. TR: 36–40 inches long; weighs 1–2 pounds. PR: 14–22 inches long; weighs 5½ ounces

Habitat: EDR: Elevated areas near floodplains and swamps, forests, dunes. TR: Lowland forests near water. PR: Scrublands, coastal areas, forests, swamps

Range: They can be found across much of the southeastern US. These rattlesnake species can be found throughout much of the Carolinas. The pygmy and eastern diamondback rattlesnakes have the most southern range.

Food: EDR: Small mammals, birds. TR: Rabbits, squirrels, rats, mice, birds, other snakes, lizards, and frogs. PR: Insects, small mammals, frogs, and lizards

Mating: September to January; mating occurs in the summer and fall. Males display a courtship "dance."

Nest: The mother gives birth in a burrow or hollow log.

Eggs: They are ovoviviparous, which means the eggs hatch inside of the female and snakes are born live.

Young: EDR: 6–21 snakelets are born; around 15 inches long. TR: Females give birth to 12 or more young; around 10–18 inches long. PR: Give birth to 1–12 young

Predators: Coyotes, humans, bobcats, skunks, foxes, hawks, and owls; king snakes, indigo snakes, and cottonmouths

Eastern diamondback: Brown, yellow, or tan, with black, gray, or brownish diamond. Timber: Gray, brown, or pink, with brown or orange stripes. Pygmy: Gray to black with hints of orange, and brown lines down the back. All have catlike pupils.

Did you know?

While the southern toad has warts on it, you cannot get warts from touching it. Toads are toxic (but not to humans); they have two parotid glands—one behind each eye that produces a toxin called bufotoxin *(Byu-fa-tox-in)* they release to prevent predators from eating them. Another way they prevent themselves from being eaten is to suck in air, causing their bodies to puff up and seem larger than what they actually are.

Most Active

Hibernates

Southern Toad

Anaxyrus terrestris

Size: 1½–4 inches long; weighs 1½–2 ounces

Habitat: Forests, suburban areas, swamps, farm fields, marshes, and other wetlands

Range: They are found throughout most of the southeastern United States from as far west as Louisiana and eastward to Georgia. They are found as far north as southern Virgina and as far south as Florida. In South Carolina, they are found in the coastal plain area, as well as in the Piedmont Plateau and Blue Ridge Mountains areas of the state in isolated populations.

Food: Insects such as ants, bees, beetles, and crickets; they also feed on algae, worms, snails, and dead animals (carrion).

Mating: February to October

Nest: No nest

Eggs: 2,500–4,000 jelly-like eggs are laid in a long coil strand in bodies of water.

Young: Eggs hatch 2–4 days after laying. They will stay in the tadpole stage for 30–55 days. It takes 2–3 years to reach reproductive maturity.

Predators: Hognoses and other snakes, raccoons, giant water bugs, turtles, and birds; as tadpoles: beetles, crawfish, birds, and dragonfly larvae

Southern toads are mostly brown but can also appear reddish to clay-colored, black, and gray with various dark spots and blotches on their back. They have a paler underbody, and their skin is dry. Males are smaller than females and have a darker-colored throat during the breeding season.

Did you know?

Spotted salamanders are also known as mole salamanders because they spend most of their time underground in burrows, only coming above the surface to eat and breed. Spotted salamanders make a toxin that tastes nasty to predators. They may have a symbiotic relationship (meaning they help each other) with algae. The algae produce oxygen for the salamander eggs while the eggs offer protection for the algae.

Most Active

Hibernates

Spotted Salamander

Ambystoma maculatum

Size: 6–10 inches long; weighs ½ ounce

Habitat: Forest areas with ponds

Range: They can be found from Canada to the eastern United States, as far north as Maine, as far south as Georgia, and as far west as Texas. In North Carolina, this species is rare in the Coastal Plain and most common in the eastern Piedmont region.

Food: Worms, insects, snails, slugs, millipedes, spiders, and other salamanders; they eat algae before metamorphosis.

Mating: March to April

Nest: No nest is built; egg masses are laid directly in ponds.

Eggs: Females lay one or more jelly-like egg mass, with each mass containing about 100–200 eggs.

Young: Eggs will hatch within a month or two after laying. The larvae are brown to yellowish, with external gills and spots. In 2–4 months, they absorb their gills and leave the water.

Predators: Birds, fish, skunks, turtles, snakes, and raccoons

Spotted salamanders are large stout salamanders that spend most of their lives underground. They come in shades of gray, black, or brown on the topside and gray on the underside. Running along each side are two uneven rows of yellow spots. These spots start at the head and run to the tip of the salamander's tail. Females are larger than males and have brighter spots.

Glossary

Adaptation—An animal's physical (outward) or behavioral (inward) adjustment to changes in the environment.

Amphibian—A small animal with a backbone, moist skin, and no scales. Most amphibians start out as an egg, live at least part of their life in water, and finish life as a land dweller.

Biome—A part or region of Earth that has a particular type of climate and animals and plants that adapted to live in the area.

Bird—A group of animals that all have two legs and feet, a beak, feathers, and wings; while not all birds fly, all birds lay eggs.

Brood—A group of young birds that hatch at the same time and with the same mother.

Carnivore—An animal that primarily eats other animals.

Clutch—The number of eggs an animal lays during one nesting period; an animal can lay more than one clutch each season.

Crepuscular—The hours before sunset or just after sunrise; some animals have adapted to be most active during these low-light times.

Diurnal—During the day; many animals are most active during the daytime.

Ecosystem—A group of animals and plants that interact with each other and the physical area that they live in.

Evolution—A process of change in a species or a group of animals that are all the same kind; evolution happens over several generations or in a group of animals living around the same time; evolution happens through adaptation, or physical and biological changes to better fit the environment over time.

Fledgling—A baby bird that has developed flight feathers and has left the nest.

Gestation—The length of time a developing mammal is carried in its mother's womb.

Herbivore—An animal that primarily eats plants.

Hibernation—A survival strategy or process where animals "slow down" and go into a long period of reduced activity to survive winter or seasonal changes; during hibernation, activities like feeding, breathing, and converting food to energy all stop.

Insectivore—An animal whose diet consists of insects.

Incubate—When a bird warms eggs by sitting on them

Invasive—A non-native animal that outcompetes native animals in a particular area, harming the environment.

Mammal—An air-breathing, warm-blooded, fur- or hair-covered animal with a backbone. All mammals produce milk and usually give birth to live young.

Migration—When animals move from one area to another. Migration usually occurs seasonally, but it can also happen due to biological processes, such as breeding.

Molt—When animals shed or drop their skin, feathers, or shell.

Nocturnal—At night; many animals are most active at night.

Piscivore—An animal that eats mainly fish.

Predator—An animal that hunts (and eats) other animals.

Raptor—A group of birds that all have a curved beak and sharp talons; they hunt or feed on other animals. Also known as a bird of prey.

Reptile—An egg-laying, air-breathing, cold-blooded animal that has a backbone and skin made of scales, which crawls on its belly or uses stubby legs to get around.

Scat—The waste product that animals release from their bodies; another word for it is poop or droppings.

Talon—The claw on the feet seen on raptors and birds of prey.

Torpor—A form of hibernation in which an animal slows down its breathing and heart rate; torpor ranges from a few hours at a time to a whole day; torpor does not involve a deep sleep.

Checklist

Mammals

- [ ] American Beaver
- [ ] Big Brown Bat
- [ ] Black Bear
- [ ] Coyote
- [ ] Eastern Chipmunk
- [ ] Eastern Cottontail
- [ ] Eastern Fox Squirrel
- [ ] Eastern Gray Squirrel
- [ ] Elk
- [ ] Gray Fox
- [ ] Long-tailed Weasel
- [ ] Mink
- [ ] Northern Raccoon
- [ ] Northern River Otter
- [ ] Northern/Southern Flying Squirrel
- [ ] Red Fox
- [ ] Red Wolf
- [ ] Tri-colored Bat
- [ ] Virginia Opossum
- [ ] White-tailed Deer

Birds

- [ ] Anhinga
- [ ] Bald Eagle
- [ ] Barred Owl
- [ ] Belted Kingfisher
- [ ] Black Skimmer
- [ ] Black Vulture/ Turkey Vulture
- [ ] Carolina Wren
- [ ] Double-crested Cormorant
- [ ] Eastern Towhee
- [ ] Eastern Whip-poor-will
- [ ] Golden-winged Warbler
- [ ] Great Blue Heron
- [ ] Great Horned Owl
- [ ] Mallard
- [ ] Northern Bobwhite
- [ ] Northern Cardinal
- [ ] Northern Mockingbird
- [ ] Osprey
- [ ] Painted Bunting
- [ ] Purple Gallinule

- [ ] Red-tailed Hawk/ Red-shouldered Hawk
- [ ] Sandhill Crane
- [ ] White Ibis
- [ ] Wild Turkey
- [ ] Wood Stork

Reptiles and Amphibians

- [ ] American Alligator
- [ ] Common Snapping Turtle
- [ ] Diamondback Terrapin
- [ ] Eastern Box Turtle
- [ ] Eastern Copperhead
- [ ] Eastern Coral Snake
- [ ] Eastern Garter Snake
- [ ] Eastern Glass Lizard
- [ ] Eastern Hognose Snake
- [ ] Eastern King Snake
- [ ] Eastern Tiger Salamander
- [ ] Gopher Tortoise
- [ ] Green Anole
- [ ] Loggerhead Sea Turtle/ Green Sea Turtle
- [ ] Northern Watersnake
- [ ] Rattlesnakes
- [ ] Southern Toad
- [ ] Spotted Salamander

The Art of Conservation®

Featuring two signature programs, The Songbird Art Contest™ and The Fish Art Contest®, the Art of Conservation programs celebrate the arts as a cornerstone to conservation. To enter, youth artists create an original hand-drawn illustration and written essay, story, or poem synthesizing what they have learned. The contests are FREE to enter and open to students in K-12. For program updates, rules, guidelines, and entry forms, visit: www.TheArtofConservation.org.

The Fish Art Contest® introduces youth to the wonders of fish, the joy of fishing, and the importance of aquatic conservation. The Fish Art Contest uses art, science, and creative writing to foster connections to the outdoors and inspire the next generation of stewards. Participants are encouraged to use the Fish On! lesson plan, then submit an original, handmade piece of artwork to compete for prizes and international recognition.

The Songbird Art Contest® explores the wonders and species diversity of North American songbirds. Raising awareness and educating the public on bird conservation, the Songbird program builds stewardship, encourages outdoors participation, and promotes the discovery of nature.

Photo Credits

Stewart Ragan: 144
Silhouettes and tracks by Anthony Hertzel unless otherwise noted.
s=silhouette

All images used under license from Shutterstock.com:
John L. Absher: 68, 86; **ace03:** footer burst; **Robert Adami:** 78; **Agami Photo Agency:** 61, 72, 73; **Airin.dizain:** 36s; **Md. Ershad Ali:** 24; **Alpha C:** 24s; **Lukasz Antoniszyn:** 35; **Archaeopteryx Tours:** 91; **AS project:** 8 (NC flag); **Bonnie Taylor Barry:** 82, 88, 89; **basel101658:** 34s; **Bennian:** 8 (SC seal); **Joan Blom:** 81; **Karel Bock:** 45; **Brad Boland:** 126; **Todd Boland:** 99; **Steve Byland:** 85, 131; **Mark Castiglia:** 17; **Phoo Chan:** 67; **Christopher T Photography:** 64; **Romuald Cisakowski:** 32; **cooky_luvs:** 127; **Mircea Costina:** 50, 115; **Creeping Things:** 110; **Sandi Cullifer:** 94; **Chase D'animulls:** 117; **Gerald A. DeBoer:** 49; **Danita Delimont:** 30, 80, 133; **DarAnna:** 79; **DnDavis:** 77; **Dominate Studio:** 12s; **Dennis W Donohue:** 22; **Ian Duffield:** 92; **J.A. Dunbar:** 95; **Kozyreva Elena:** 32s; **Eroshka:** 48s; **Will Falcon:** 8 (loggerhead sea turtle); **Deborah Ferrin:** 19; **Frank Fichtmueller:** 13; **Florida Stock:** 54; **Jiri Foltyn:** 21; **FotoRequest:** 56, 60; **Gallinago_media:** 42s; **Ghost Bear:** 33; **Glass and Nature:** 41; **Edwin Godinho:** 26; **Leonardo Gonzalez:** 129; **Amanda Guercio:** 118; **Elliotte Rusty Harold:** 38; **Harry Collins Photography:** 42, 59; **Sarah Heinitz:** 8 (Carolina wren); **Hrach Hovhannisyan:** 8 (honey bee); **Heather L. Hubbard:** 71; **Malachi Ives:** 57; **Jukka Jantunen:** 40; **Matt Jeppson:** 123, 137; **Joseph Scott Photography:** 75; **Tory Kallman:** 98; **Breck P. Kent:** 100; **Iftikhar Ahmad Khan:** 44; **Heiko Kiera:** 132; **Francisco Martinez Lanzas:** 34; **Brian Lasenby:** 58, 104; **Sakis Lazarides:** 128; **lazyllama:** 8 (sabal palemetto); **leisuretime70:** 107; **L-N:** 37; **Amy Lutz:** 8 (white-tailed deer); **mamita:** 18s; **Don Mammoser:** 53, 93, 97; **Wilfred Marissen:** 90; **Karl R. Martin:** 74; **Kazakova Maryia:** 11 (ground nest); **Brittany Mason:** 106; **Martin Mecnarowski:** 87; **Elly Miller:** 55; **Miloje:** background/inset burst; **Michael Minion:** 70; **Christian Musat:** 12; **nialat:** 39; **Matthew L Niemiller:** 15; **OBX Wildlife:** 121; **Jay Ondreicka:** 14, 46, 47, 111, 112, 113, 116, 119, 120, 122, 130; **Paul Reeves Photography:** 36, 65, 69; **Nick Pecker:** 48; **Angela N Perryman:** 27; **pichayasri:** 11 (platform nest), 11 (suitcase); **Dimitrios Pippis:** 109; **gary powell:** 63; **predragilievski:** 28s; **psmphotography:** 125; **Rabbitti:** 23; **Suzanne Renfrow:** 124; **RICIfoto:** 103; **Wasan Ritthawon:** 8 (SC flag); **Leena Robinson:** 25; **Jason Patrick Ross:** 114; **Menno Schaefer:** 43; **George Schmiesing:** 20; **Jim Schwabel:** 102; **SCStock:** 16; **Shoriful_is:** 83; **Benjamin Simeneta:** 105; **SofiaV:** 11 (cavity nest); **spacaj:** 96; **sreewing:** 28t; **Rostislav Stach:** 28, 29; **Stock for you:** 8 (pine); **stopkin:** 16s; **Stubblefield Photography:** 84; **Cecilie Bergan Stuedal:** 8 (eastern gray squirrel); **Sunshower Shots:** 62; **T_Dub0v:** 11 (cup nest); **Paul Tessier:** 51; **Thomas Torget:** 18, 31; **Suzanne Tucker:** 108; **vectoric:** 10 (basketball); **Viktorya170377:** 20s; **Hans Wagemaker:** 52; **Chuck W Walker:** 101; **Liz Weber:** 134, 135; **w e s o m e 24:** 22s; **Mike Wilhelm:** 8 (spotted salamander), 136; **Wirestock Creators:** 8 (eastern box turtle), 8 (northern cardinal), 66; **ya_mayka:** 38s; **yongsheng chen:** 76

About the Author

Alex Troutman is a wildlife biologist, birder, nature enthusiast, and science communicator from Austell, Georgia. He has a passion for sharing the wonders of nature and introducing the younger generation to the outdoors. He holds both a bachelor's degree and a master's degree in biology from Georgia Southern University (the Real GSU), with a focus in conservation. Alex knows what it feels like not to see individuals who look like you (or come from a similar background) doing the things you enjoy or working in the career that you aspire to be in. He makes a point to be that representation for the younger generation, ensuring that kids have exposure to the careers they are interested in and to the diverse scientists working in those careers.

Alex is the co-organizer of several Black in X weeks, including Black Birders Week, Black Mammalogists Week, and Black in Marine Science Week. This movement encourages diversity in nature, the celebration of Black individual scientists, awareness of Black nature enthusiasts, and diversity in STEAM fields.

ABOUT ADVENTUREKEEN

We are an independent nature and outdoor activity publisher. Our founding dates back more than 40 years, guided then and now by our love of being in the woods and on the water, by our passion for reading and books, and by the sense of wonder and discovery made possible by spending time recreating outdoors in beautiful places. It is our mission to share that wonder and fun with our readers, especially with those who haven't yet experienced all the physical and mental health benefits that nature and outdoor activity can bring. #bewellbeoutdoors